How To Be Alone Without Feeling Lonely

Dr. Ida Greene

ISBN 1-881165-26-4
Library of Congress Card Catalog Number:

**ATTENTION COLLEGES AND UNIVERSITIES,
CORPORATIONS, and PROFESSIONAL
ORGANIZATIONS**:

Quantity discounts are available on bulk purchases of this
book for educational training purposes, fund raising, or gift
giving. For information contact: **P. S. I. Publishers, 2910
Baily Avenue, San Diego, CA 92105 (619) 262-9951.**

Contents

**Introduction -
Traveling the Journey of Life Alone**   **4**

**Chapter 1
The Impact of Living Alone, Chronic Illness**   **8**

**Chapter 2
The Purpose of Life**   **32**

**Chapter 3
The Road Less Traveled**   **48**

**Chapter 4
How to Be Alone Without Feeling Lonely**   **72**

Introduction
Traveling the Journey of Life Alone

Even though I have been married twice, I have traveled the road of singleness as an individual longer than I have as a partner or couple. My home is in Pensacola Florida. I went to Chicago to live with my aunt Ida, who was a licensed Vocational Nurse, because I wanted go to nursing school to become a Registered Nurse, which I did. After finishing nursing school, I rented a room with a lady from my church in Chicago, dated, worked, and attended DePaul University. I became tired of dating and decided that I wanted to be married. I made my wish known to my dad, and he went to work to find me a husband. My dad found Theodis White, the young man who took me to the 12th grade prom. He had moved to San Diego California to go into the Marines. My dad gave him my phone number, and he started calling me three to four times a week at 6 am telling me that he would be my future husband.

I got tired of the phone calls and decided to visit him in San Diego for one week to stop the phone calls and get to know him better. To my surprise, this quiet, shy young man was a master salesman on getting what he wanted, and I returned to Chicago with an engagement ring. I requested that we become engaged for a year; six months later I was planning my marriage and my move to San Diego California. My husband was employed as a custodian at San Diego State College. I worked the 3-11 pm shift as a nurse, and he worked the day shift, so we did not see a lot of each other except when sleeping.

Two years after my marriage, we moved to San Jose California where my husband had his work transferred. My girlfriend from Chicago Illinois came to visit us and noticed my husband's obsession and strange paranoid behavior. Once I accepted that my husband was having a mental and emotional breakdown, I phoned his uncle to come help us move back to San Diego.

I discovered later that his family knew that he had mental issues that were masked by his quietness, but they did not tell me because they thought marriage would solve his problem. Once we moved back to San Diego, I started working again as a psychiatric nurse and took him to see one of the hospital psychiatrists who admitted him to the hospital where I worked for depression due to paranoid schizophrenia. I left that hospital to work at San Diego County Mental Health, and due to the financial burden of his shock therapy treatments, I had to transfer him to the hospital where I worked as a psychiatric charge nurse. I was placed on the women's unit so that my husband could be admitted to the male unit where I was working.

Eventually he was admitted to a state hospital for long term care. His family in Florida decided they wanted to take care of him in their home. He contracted pneumonia and died in his parent's home in Pensacola Florida. I had no relatives in San Diego and was afraid to live alone, so spent the night at one of my co-workers home. One of the night nurses gave me a puppy to keep me company. I kept Sparky in a box, beside my bed.

I was very angry with my husband for dying on me, abandoning me and leaving me to live alone in San Diego. I went to my pastor and told him we needed a group for divorced people. He suggested I start a singles group, so I did. I started the first Singles Club in San Diego. I did a lot of advertising in Los Angeles, and my group was the place for people from out of town to visit. One of the couples in my group even got married.

These were trying times for me, so I went back to college to get my Bachelors degree in Psychology and my Masters degree in Counseling. I submerged myself into my studies to forget about my troubles even though I felt very alone at the time.

Then one night, I went out to a nightclub with my cousin who had just moved to San Diego, to help her find a date and left the club with a date for myself. He took me home that Saturday night. The next day when I left church, he was parked outside waiting for me. Every night when I got off from work as a psychiatric nurse, on the 3 -11 pm shift, he was parked outside my house waiting for me at 1 am. We talked for hours, sometimes until 5 am. We dated for eight months as he worked out of town as a truck driver. He missed me, wanted to move in to live with me, but I said not unless I was married. So we got married. This was one of the red flag signs of domestic violence—a short courtship.

Later, I found out that he had a problem with alcohol, had a violent temper and had a borderline personality disorder. These were signs I did not see because I was in love and wanted to believe that I was using good judgment, even though I was not at the time due to the isolation of us as a couple.

During our five-year marriage of domestic violence, we went to marriage counseling and a couples encounter group to deal with his extreme jealousy, controlling behavior and physical abuse of me. After he hit me the first time, I dismissed it. When he hit me the second time, I fought back and got a big black and blue mark under my eye. I was ashamed to go to work looking like that, so I stayed home from work and said nothing to anyone at work about the abuse I encountered by my husband—another red flag sign of domestic violence. He said he was sorry for hitting me and promised me that if he hit me again he would cut off his right hand. I believed him and went back to the relationship. When he hit me for a third time, I realized that he did not cut off his hand, and that he could not help himself. I felt angry, helpless and alone. His body build was bigger than mine, plus he was an ex-boxer, so I realized I was in a relationship losing game. I made up my mind that if he ever hit me again, I was going to kill him. I felt powerless to help myself.

He did hit me again, and the anger and resentment I had for him started to well up inside me. I started thinking on a daily basis of how I could kill him. I realized this was premeditated murder and the thought of going to prison, forced me to divorce him, which was a long process of putting him out of the house and letting him come back again. I had no family in San Diego, so I had a lot of fear about living in a house by myself, which I had never done before. I had two big fears: a fear of letting go my failed marriage and a bigger fear of being alone again, which was very traumatic for me after my first husband died.

At the time I had a foster son living with me, and I was torn that he might need a father figure. I finally made the decision to leave my husband after six or more consultations with my attorney, who told me that she was going to drop my case if I canceled my divorce proceedings one more time. So I moved myself and my son out of the house and went to live with one of my psychiatric nurse co-workers while I filed for my divorce and got a restraining order against my husband. My husband did not easily accept my decision to leave him. I was stalked on my job. He broke the door off the hinges and came into my home in the presence of one my neighbors, a church member who was visiting to see if I was alright. He took the keys to my car and took off from the house. I called the police who arrested him. He went to court and the judge gave him 90 days in jail. There was still a lot of emotional abuse in our relationship. After he got out of jail, he took me to court to try to get me to give him alimony, because I was now working as a school teacher and made more money than him. He was not successful in his efforts to have me pay him alimony.

He told me that if he ever saw me with another man, he would kill both me and the man. This threat put a fear in me that stayed with me for many years. It helped me to make my decision to live alone and to begin living as a single person, which I have done for the past 20 years. In looking back, I can see that I was afraid to be alone and live alone. In this book I will take you on my journey of how I learned "How to Be Alone Without Feeling Lonely".

Chapter 1
The Impact of Living Alone, Violence and Chronic Illness

Living alone has its liabilities, because when you get sick you have no one to look after you. It can be scary if you get ill, fall or need to get to the hospital and you are living alone. A growing body of science is consistently linking violence (the experience with and/or fear of violence) with risk for and incidence of a range of serious physical health problems. There is a correlation between fear, worry and anxiety one may experience about living alone or worrying about who will take care of them. Sometime people remain in toxic abusive relationships, because they have fears about their health or living alone. Violence shows up in many ways through our interactions with others in our work or personal life. Violence and abuse can be physical, verbal or emotional.

While it has been long understood that violence has implications for emotional and physical injury, it is only relatively recently that we are beginning to recognize the longer-term effects that reap an extensive toll on the broader health status of individuals, families and communities. These health consequences include asthma, significant alteration of healthy eating and activity, heart disease, hypertension, ulcers, gastrointestinal disorders, diabetes, neurological and musculoskeletal diseases and lung disease. The effects of violence on health are a consequence of the physical, biological, environmental, social, behavioral and emotional changes that violence imposes on all of us.

Listed below are a few of the health challenges that are related to having feelings about being alone, living alone or being the victim of violence or abuse. This information is shared to inform you, not to frighten you. Living alone like everything else has pro and con factors.

Asthma

• Adults with asthma who had witnessed violence in their neighborhoods were twice as likely to visit the hospital for asthma, than those without exposure to violence.

• Children of mothers experiencing intimate partner violence have a two-fold increased risk of developing asthma than those not exposed to violence.

• In a study of 7 cities across the U.S., increased exposure to violence predicted higher number of days with significant symptoms related to asthma; the greater the exposure, the greater the number of symptomatic days.

• Chicago children from neighborhoods with moderate to serious problems with violence were about 60 percent more likely to develop asthma than children from less violent neighborhoods.

• Exposure and/or fear of violence is associated with both increased prevalence of and severity of asthma, particularly among children ages 1-6. This appears to be the case across cultural and geographic boundaries. Risk factors from violence that relate to asthma include:

• Enhancement of the effects of other asthma risk factors, e.g. air pollution. The exposure to violence appears synergistic with exposure to air pollution in increasing the risk for developing asthma.

• Increased stress and anxiety, when they are known to trigger and exacerbate asthma.

• Parental stress/anxiety affecting compliance and medical follow up.

• Reduced physical activity affecting overall health and lung function.

• Physically deteriorated community environments enhancing exposure to allergens.

Other Chronic Illnesses
• Adults reporting exposure to violence as children had increased likelihood of a number of chronic health conditions compared to those without such exposures, especially if their experience involved multiple forms of violence exposures (ischemic heart disease 2.2x, cancer 1.9x, stroke 2.4x, chronic obstructive lung disease 3.9x, diabetes 1.6x, hepatitis 2.4x).

• Both men and women who experienced intimate partner violence had an increased risk of developing a chronic disease than those not exposed.

• There is a significantly higher likelihood of engaging in behaviors known to contribute to chronic illness behaviors (smoking, eating disorders, substance abuse, decreased physical activity) for those who have been exposed to one or more of the range of types of interpersonal violence (e.g. child abuse, sexual assault, family violence, community violence).

• Mothers with high exposure to community violence were twice as likely to report poorer health, smoking and poor sleep habits. Research, as well as clinical experience, has identified a broad range of chronic illnesses that are either brought on by exposure to violence or are in some way exacerbated as a consequence of violence.

Most of these studies have looked at multiple health consequences of exposure to violence rather than focusing on a single disease. A brief list of disorders associated with experiencing violence (child abuse, family violence, community violence are all implicated) includes:

• Heart disease and hypertension

• Ulcers and other gastrointestinal disturbances

• Diabetes

• Neurological and musculoskeletal diseases

• Lung disease including asthma and chronic obstructive pulmonary disease (COPD)

Implications for Healthy Eating and Activity

• Children of women who report chronic intimate partner violence are 1.8 times more likely to be more obese than other children; the effect is magnified for families living in unsafe neighborhoods.

• Researchers have found that women who perceive their neighborhoods to be unsafe are 25 percent more likely to be obese.

• Children of parents who perceived their neighborhood as unsafe were 4 times more likely to be overweight than those of parents who perceived their neighborhood as safe.

• Mothers with high exposure to neighborhood violence were twice as likely to report never exercising.

• Persons who described their neighborhood as not at all safe were nearly three times more likely to be physically inactive than those describing their neighborhood as extremely safe. Exposure to and fear of violence of all types (domestic, interpersonal, community) creates barriers to healthy eating and behavior. This relationship appears to be the consequence of multiple effects of violence on communities, individuals and populations.

Effects on Communities
• Reduced investment in community resources including parks and recreation facilities and other activities that promote healthy activity.

• Reluctance for food related resources such as supermarkets to enter the community, reducing access to healthy foods.

Effects on Individuals and Populations

• Reduced physical activity/increased sedentary time.

• Increased use of processed and unhealthy food due to decreased access to food choices.

• Reduce optimism, increased anxiety and other emotional consequences affecting motivation for healthy living and activity.

• Parental restriction of activity of children, especially related to the outdoors.

We must recognize and understand that all forms of abuse or violence in the family take a serious toll on the general health and well-being of all community members. Every system in the body, from our hearts to our lungs to our intestines to our nervous systems, can be affected in harmful ways by our feelings and emotions. Many of the behaviors that contribute to poor health can be increased, further affecting how we feel and function. Therefore it is to our benefit when we understand the many factors that influence our physical as well as mental health. Self-knowledge is the key to understanding all the factors that can affect us like the environment, emotional trauma, abuse, violence and its relationship to our well-being. We are energetic, emotional and feeling human beings.

There are many shades of the feelings we experience that negatively affect our feelings and emotion like fear or anger. Men's language for these feelings is usually less well-developed than female's, however we all have these feelings. The only way most of us learn how to label our different feelings is by being around other people who can give us feedback.

Our feeling states affect every part of our life. For example, when you were a baby you didn't know the names of the different colors. Someone kept telling you that the sky was blue and that the fire engine was red. You learned, after more practice, that red had many different shades: scarlet is different from pink, and maroon is not quite the same as burgundy. The same is true for feelings. The different levels and shades of anger may range from irritated and frustrated to furious and enraged.

Below is a list of some of our common feelings.

However we have four primary feelings:
1. **Sad**
2. **Joy**
3. **Fear (anxiety)**
4. **Anger**

Take the test now. See if you can classify the feelings below into one of the four major feeling categories. Put a number by the feelings, then state to the right of the feeling if you felt that feeling today, this week or this month.

	Today	This Week	This Month
•excited			
•tender			
•sad			
•lonely			
•edgy			
•frustrated			
•frightened			
•contented			
•depressed			
•timid			
•hurt			
•jealous			
•loving			
•elated			
•happy			

Many people include a fifth feeling category, known as shame or humiliation. Some feelings may not fit neatly into only one category. The more familiar you are with these different feeling states, the more power you will have over your own experiences and reactions. Today in our society, violence is taking a toll on the way we show love, affection and intimacy in all our relationships, our family unity and our emotional stability.

Violence also has a great impact on our self-esteem. It lowers our self-esteem and our self-worth and it creates an environment where a person can become a victim of domestic violence and emotional abuse. These are some of the signs of low self-esteem that if not addressed can allow you to feel abused or become a victim of domestic violence or verbal abuse.

Low Self-Esteem

Learned Behavior Pattern of Aggressive Acts

1.   Aggressive Vital/Emotional Attacking Behaviors. This can be an inherited trait or a behavior a child learns from emulating one of their parents.

2.   Rigid Restrictive Environment. A rigid restrictive environment is something a child learns from a parent or adapts to as a result of living with or being around a rigid person or environment. We become like the environment we are exposed to on a daily basis.

3.   Non-Supportive Negative Reinforcement. A child's self-esteem and personality is negatively affected when they live a non-supportive negative reinforcement environment.

4.   Critical, Rejecting, Assaulter Verbal Parental Abuse. This kind of abuse or abusive person can and will destroy the self-esteem and self-worth of a child or an adult who does not believe in themselves or has low self-esteem or low self-worth.

5.   Social Emotional Delay

a. Developmental Emotional Social Blocking. Social emotional blocking occurs when there is faulty parenting, ineffective parenting or parents who are developmentally delayed.

b. Oppositional Defiant Behaviors. This behavior is often seen in children with Attention Deficit Hyper Active disorder. The person or child needs to be evaluated by a Mental Health Professional to rule out this diagnosis and plan of action created to help them correct this behavioral flaw.

c. Emotional Reflection, Abuse. The person or child needs to be evaluated by a Mental Health Professional to determine the cause of this behavior. Emotional reflection occurs when someone identifies with and creates a mindset or belief that has little or no value to themselves or to the world.

d. Isolation/Non-Acceptance Act of Abuse. Isolation can cause a person to be shy and behave in a non-communicative manner. It is always healthy when someone says or has a non-acceptance of abuse. Abuse negatively impacts our self-esteem. However, when we are isolated and only receive or hear negative feedback about ourselves on a continuous basis, we soon come to believe the negative ideas we hold about us rather than the positive beliefs we want to hold. Here are some positive self-esteem concepts you want to remember.

Positive Self-Esteem Concepts

✓ The person takes care for what is best for them.

✓ Compassion is to have sympathy and empathy for the feelings and predicaments of others.

✓ To love is to open your heart to the faults, shortcomings and mistakes of others and do the same for yourself. Suspend your judgment.

✓ Commitment allows you to let go of your fears of what could happen and stay around to see what happens, and to work through the rough waters to get to the other side of the situation on matters of concern.

✓ Love means never having to say you are sorry.

✓ You know others love you by the way they respect you, take care of your feelings and are willing to put forth the effort to correct any perception of lack of caring or intention to hurt you.

✓ People who love you watch what they say and do to you and avoid doing or saying things they feel might hurt, offend or demean you or your character.

✓ Independence of thought and actions is strength of character.

✓ Compassion means to release all judgment about yourself and others and focus on the love, light and good that is within everyone including you.

✓ Love yourself and others and every situation no matter what the outward appearance may be.

✓ Integrity is doing the right thing all the time.

✓ To increase your self-esteem, stand up for what you believe is right.

✓ Persons with high self-esteem believe in themselves and in their ability to provide and take care of themselves. They do not rely on others to provide or take care of them.

✓ Persons with high self-esteem know that they are worthy of Spirit's love for them. Regardless of what they may have done, they are given another chance to correct their faults and shortcomings.

✓ Persons with high self-esteem work diligently to be independent of the thoughts, feelings, attitude and negative beliefs others may sometimes hold about them.

Believing In Yourself
Important Points to Remember

➢ Set a goal and note a timetable for completion.
➢ Prioritize your goals; add things that help and discard those that hinder.
➢ Feed yourself daily with positive information, and minimize, if not eliminate, any negative influences.
➢ Stay committed to your goals and commitments.
➢ Remain disciplined and diligent.
➢ Remain balanced spiritually, economically, emotionally and physically.
➢ Stay focused on your goal, not your challenge.

How to Read the Body Language of Others

This has many benefits for us in our personal as well as professional life, like:

- We see the **true emotions** of others by looking at their faces.
- You can detect up to 80 percent of the **lies** you hear in business meetings.
- Lead **effective conversations** based on non-verbal clues.

- Understand how body language impacts **authentic communication.**
- Use authentic communication to effectively **share a message.**
- Understand why non-verbal and verbal **alignment** is important to authentic communication.

We are relationship oriented, therefore we are affected by everyone, including the things people say and do in our presence especially if they say it to us, or the way they behave in a manner that is offensive or abusive in nature. It is easy for us to experience abuse without knowing it ever happened. Emotional abuse is very common. Most physically abused people are attracted to and will enter into an abusive relationships, or be self-abusive. We need to be aware of this, because it is part of the process on how we change our old beliefs, thoughts, behavior patterns and concepts to create a new behavior pattern or mindset.

If a person heard in the past that they were no good at something, they will come to accept and believe the words of the person who said those words to them. After hearing the self-destructive message over a long period of time by their parents, caretaker or guardian, a child or an adult will come to believe this is the truth about them. When we are living with someone or are in an intimate relationship, we will accept and take on the old self-depreciating words of identification we heard in the past which seemed at the time to be words of affection and love. So in the future when the person hears the words "you are no good," they hear words of love. To them it seems like love, even though they are not really words of love. The person then comes to believe the words they have heard in the past, because through repetition, their mind was programmed and they soon become convinced they are worthless because of the words said to them over and again: that they had no value as a person and therefore they are defective. I call this emotional brainwashing and psychological or emotional abuse, which can happen to us without our knowing this has occurred. One way to understand how you are being treated by others is to see yourself through the eyes of a child.

Think of yourself as a child with infantile, omnipotent ideas. Children tend to blame themselves for what happened to them in their family life. They take the blame, so their distorted low self-worth and low self-belief is reinforced and carried with them into their adult life with the same negative and self-defeating beliefs patterns they will play out in their life as an adult.

What happened to you as a child is not your fault. You cannot change anything about your past, so you must learn to embrace it, love it or attempt to correct the false beliefs you heard as a child and move on in a positive direction in the future. What happened in your past may be similar to what is happening to you in the present. However, the past is never equal to what is happening to you in the present. Similar is not equal, so you do not need to abuse yourself now or in the future. As a child you may have had mean things said to you that you thought were words of love or affection. Once you become aware of this difference it is up to you to make a change in your behavior.

I remember when I was young I was clumsy and I always dropped or broke the glasses or dishes. My dad would remark, "That is so stupid." I thought I was stupid even though that was not what he meant. I never asked for clarification, and for many years I felt that I was dumb and stupid. Then I would repeat the same thing in my mind to myself except, I would say, "You are stupid" mentally to myself. It was not until many years later when I was in a therapeutic group and I was expressing this in the group that I got the clarification, which was I had taken the words "That is stupid" to mean "I was stupid." Sometimes we can misinterpret what we hear, so it is always a good idea to get into therapy or get therapeutic coaching or objective feedback from someone.

We can all use some corrective insight into how we perceived our childhood. There may have been actual abuse in our childhood, or it could be our interpretation of the abuse we felt that occurred to us as a child. If you were verbally abused as a child, you do not want to continue to abuse yourself. Don't take over where the last person left off. Do you know how to cope with verbal abuse?

How to Cope with Verbally Abusive People

Verbal abuse in the workplace, or anywhere else, is not something you want to tolerate. You want to look for ways to prevent verbal abuse and what approach you will use. People who are verbally abusive put other people on the defensive. Notice if you do this, and if so rather than trying to defend yourself, you can respond with, "What did you say? Would you repeat that again?" or "Let me write that down."

Also, you want to document the person's outbursts and ask them to provide a record of everything they are asked to do to avoid being blamed for the mistakes of someone else. Before taking drastic measures, you want to talk to the verbally offending person when he or she is calm to find how you can both communicate more effectively.

Although being the target of verbal abuse can make you want to give up, it can also be an opportunity for change to occur in the relationship. Although dealing with verbal abuse is a sensitive issue, if you are the target by someone, this can give you the push to release some of the personal baggage you have been holding back that has prevented you from reaching your greater potential or living your life to the fullest.

Always Live Life to the Fullest
A Guide to Self-Esteem
Nancye Sims

Don't let go of hope.
Hope gives you the strength to keep going when you feel like giving up.
Don't ever quit believing yourself.
As long as you believe you can,
You will have a reason for trying.
Don't let anyone hold your happiness in their hands;
Hold it in yours, so it will always be within reach.

Don't measure success or failure by material wealth,
But by how you feel;
Our feelings determine the richness of our lives.
Don't let bad moments overcome you;
Be patient and they will pass.
Don't hesitate to reach out for help;
We all need it from time to time.
Don't run away from love but towards love,
Because it is our deepest joy,
Don't wait for what you want to come to you.
Go after it with all that you are, knowing that life will meet you halfway.
Don't feel like you've lost, when plans and dreams fall short of your hopes.
Anytime you learn something new
About yourself or about life,
You have progressed.
Don't do anything that takes away from your self-respect.
Feeling good about yourself,
Is essential to feeling good about life,
Don't ever forget how to laugh
Or be too proud to cry
It is by doing both that we live life to its fullest.

Symptoms of Low Self-Esteem
Are You an Eating Disorder Codependent?

Use this questionnaire from *Fat is a Family Affair* to evaluate the extent of your involvement with an under or overeater, who could be you. Answer the questions below.

Do you force yourself to diet?

Do you threaten to leave a relationship due to your weight?

Do you check on your diet?

Do you make promises based on pounds lost or gained?

Do you hide food from an overeater?

Do you worry incessantly about being an undereater?

Have you "walked on eggshells" so as not to upset the over/undereater?

Do you throw food away so the overeater won't find it?

Have you excused the erratic, sometimes violent, mood swings resulting from sugar binges?

Do you change social circles so the overeater won't be tempted to eat?

Do you manipulate budgets to control spending on food and clothing?

Do you purchase and promote eating the "right" foods?

Do you promote gyms, health spas and miracle cures?

Do you break into emotional tirades when you catch the overeater bingeing?

Are you constantly disappointed when you see relapse?

Are you embarrassed by the over/undereater's appearance?

Do you falsely console the over/undereater when he or she is embarrassed?

Do you set up tests of willpower to tease the over/undereater?

Have you lowered your expectations of what you might like?

Does your weight fluctuate with your lived one's weight (you up, he or she down)?

Have you stopped attending to your own grooming?

Do you have many aches, pains and/or a preoccupation with health?

Are you drinking heavily, using sleeping pills or tranquillizers?

Do you soothe yourself with food?

Do you talk about the eater's body to him/her or to others?

Do you do this to yourself?

Do you feel life will be perfect if the over/undereater shapes up?

Are you grateful you are not as bad as them?

After you answer these questions, take your results to a therapist or relationship coach to help you decide if you need some guidance and direction to have a better relationship with food and/or your body. Many of us have experienced emotional violence as children, and it is still affecting our personal and interpersonal relationships today. Take the inventory now. Write down all issues which still have an influence on your behavior, actions or reactions.

ADULT CHILDREN OF EMOTIONAL VIOLENCE

A   Abandonment fears
D   Denial and delusion
U   Undifferentiated emotions
L   Loneliness and isolation
T   Thought disorders

C	Compulsive/addictive behavior
H	High-level anxiety
I	Intimacy problems
L	Loss of emotion and energy
D	Drive and needs are shamed
R	Resentment/guilt cycle
E	Emotions in shame binds
N	No expression of emotions; no talk rule
O	Overly controlling
F	False self
E	Empty and narcissistically deprived
M	Manipulating and gamey
O	Overindulged and over submitted to
T	Terrorized and tormented
I	Insatiable inner child
O	Overly perfectionistic, rigid, authoritarian
N	Needy and wanting
A	Abused physically or sexually or both
L	Lack of emotional coping skills, lack of communication skills
V	Violated emotional boundaries
I	Internalized anger, sadness, fear, joy, shame
O	Offender/victim ambiguity
L	Loss of inner self-unity
E	Enmeshed in caretaking others' feelings
N	"Now" phobic
C	Corrupted through bad modeling
E	Emotional constraint (with or without dramatic outbursts)

Taken from *Bradshaw On The Family* by John Bradshaw

Abuse is very common. What is known in the therapeutic community is that people who have been abused will enter into an abusive relationship or will be self-abusive. You want to become aware of this, because it is a very important part of how we let go of our old self-defeating thoughts, behavior patterns and concepts.

I remember in my past when I would say to myself, "You are stupid" it became a self-fulfilling prophecy without my realizing it. Then I learned this was mental self-abuse, and it was not until later that I decided I needed to change what I was saying to myself over and again in my head, so that I could improve my self-esteem and correct my self-abusive behavior patterns. I now know that others read my energy and will treat me the way that I treat and see myself. It is easy to abuse oneself without realizing it and thereby create an environment where they become a victim of domestic violence as I did.

Are You a Victim or Abuser of Domestic Violence?

Do your subordinates or co-workers run into their offices when they see you coming down the hall? If you are the office meanie, it's time to turn your behavior around. If you want to know if you're a verbally abusive boss or co-worker, look for the symptoms. This involves managing your anger, not by encouraging or expressing your anger. A sign to let you know this is happening is when you impact others in a way that produces silence, sullenness or hurt feelings.

To change your behavior, take the time to learn more about why you feel the need to strike out. "Verbal abuse is about a loss of power," says Ruth King. "It's about shame, fear, and feeling highly controlled and out of control. Usually people in these situations were victims and have now become perpetrators," she says.

Most importantly, learn to take a time out. I recommend that you start a time of quietness or meditate for 10 to 20 minutes every morning and evening. I have a meditation tape that can be ordered at

25

. Notice your thoughts and what you set your intention for each day. What do you want your day to be like? We all can be guilty of verbal abuse.

Domestic violence is a different situation. Here the abuse can be emotional, verbal or physical; it is called spousal abuse, domestic assault or domestic violence, because it occurs in intimate settings with a boyfriend, girlfriend, significant other or life partner.

In domestic assaults, one partner is beating, intimidating and terrorizing the other. It's not "mutual combat" or two people in a fist fight. It is one person dominating and controlling the other. The problem is not really woman abuse. It is spousal abuse. In approximately 90 percent of domestic assaults, the man is the perpetrator. This fact makes many of us uncomfortable, but it is no less true because of that discomfort. To end domestic violence, we must scrutinize why is it usually men who are violent in partnerships?

We must examine the historic and legal permission that men have been given to be violent in general, and to be violent towards their wives and children specifically. There are occasions where a woman batters a man. Battering does occur in lesbian and gay male relationships. Survivors of abuse in such relationships should realize that because their situation is rare or because they are in a socially unacceptable relationship, does not make it is less valid or serious. The National Domestic Violence Hotline believes that violence is unacceptable in intimate relationships and provides services to any person who has been victimized.

When there is violence in the family, all members of the family are participating in the dynamic; therefore all must change for the violence to stop. Only the perpetrator has the ability to stop the violence, because battering is a behavioral choice.

Many women who are battered make numerous attempts to change their behavior in the hopes that this will stop the abuse. This does not stop the abuse from occurring. Changes in family members' behavior will not cause or influence the batterer to be non-violent. Domestic violence is not a one-time event or an isolated incident. Battering is a pattern; it is a reign of force and terror.

Once violence begins in a relationship, it gets worse and more frequent over a period of time. Battering is not just one physical attack. It is a number of tactics (intimidation, threats, economic deprivation, psychological and sexual abuse) used repeatedly. Physical violence is one of those tactics. Experts have compared methods used by batterers to those used by terrorists to brainwash hostages. This is called the "Stockholm Syndrome."

Many battered women leave their abusers permanently, and despite many obstacles, succeed in building a life free of violence. Almost all battered women leave at least once. The perpetrator dramatically escalates his violence when a woman leaves (or tries to), because it is necessary for him to re-assert his control and ownership. Battered women are often very active and far from helpless to act on their own behalf. Their efforts often fail because the batterer continues to assault and institutions refuse to offer them protection. Violence or abuse is an impediment to one's success in life. Has your success as a man or woman been affected because of your feelings of being alone, or because of violence or abuse?

Who Is the Successful Woman?
Monroe Mohresweiser

The successful woman knows herself well,
And uses her talents wisely
With warmth in her smile, and comfort in her touch,
She lets others know, how special they are.
She thinks children are priceless,
And all nature is precious,
And asks what she can do to make the world
A safer and better place
The successful woman is not looking for success...
It finds her, while she is reaching out,

Touching lives, and sharing herself with others.

Attitude
Charles Swindoll

The longer I live, the more I realize the impact of attitude on life.
Attitude, to me, is more important than facts.
It is more important than the past, than education, than money,
than circumstances, than failure, than successes,
than what other people think or say or do.
It is more important than appearance, giftedness or skill.
It will make or break a company, a church, a home.
The remarkable thing is we have a choice every day
 regarding the attitude we will embrace for that day.
We cannot change our past.
We cannot change the fact that people will act in a certain way.
We cannot change the inevitable.
The only thing we can do is play, on the one string we have,
and that is our attitude.
I am convinced that life is 10% what happens to me
and 90% how I react to it.
And so it is with you, we are in charge of our Attitudes.

Step Into the Challenge

The more you do, the more you're able to do. Your abilities grow stronger as you use them, so your best strategy is to get busy and use them.

The feeling that you cannot do something is often powerful and can feed upon itself. The way to get beyond it is with action.

Any project you contemplate may at first seem overwhelming. That's understandable, because you haven't even taken the first step.

Once you take that first step, though, the challenge begins to feel more manageable. As soon as you actually begin the effort, you also begin to get better at doing it.

When the mountain is in the distance, it is difficult to imagine how you could climb it.

A Time for Everything

There is a Time for Everything and a Season for Every Activity under the Sun. There Is:
A time to be born and a time to die,
A time to plant and a time to uproot,
A time to wound and a time to heal,
A time to tear down and a time to build,
A time to weep and a time to laugh,
A time to mourn and a time to dance,
A time to scatter stones and a time to gather them,
A time to embrace and a time to refrain,
A time to search and a time to give up,
A time to keep and a time to throw away,
A time to tear and a time to mend,
A time to speak and a time to be silent,
A time to love and a time to not love,
A time for conflict, and a time for peace

How Far You Go In Life
George Washington Carver

How far you go in life depends on your being tender with the young,
Compassionate with the aged, sympathetic with the striving,
And tolerant of the weak and the strong,
Because someday in life you will have been all of these

Thoughts to Ponder

It may be that your sole purpose in life is simply to serve as a warning to others.

Never buy a car you can't push.

Never put both feet in your mouth at the same time, because then you won't have a leg to stand on.

Nobody cares if you can't dance well. Just get up and dance.

Since, it's the early worm that gets eaten by the bird, sleep late.

The second mouse gets the cheese.

When everything's coming your way, you're in the wrong lane.

Birthdays are good for you. The more you have, the longer you live.

You may be only one person in the world,

but you may also be the world to one person.

Some mistakes are too much fun to only make once.

We could learn a lot from crayons. Some are sharp, some are pretty and some are dull. Some have weird names,

and all are different colors, but they all have to live in the same box.

A truly happy person is one who can enjoy the scenery on a detour.

Have an awesome day and know that someone has thought about you today.

SAY YES, I CAN
Anonymous

You've all that the greatest of men have had;
Two arms, two hands, two legs, two eyes,
And a brain to us if you would be wise,
With this equipment they all began.
So start from the top and say, "I can."
Look them over, the wise and the great,
They take their food from a common plate,
And similar knives and forks they use,
With similar laces they tie their shoes,
The world considers them brave and smart,

But you've all they had when they made their start.

You can triumph and come to skill,

You can be great if you only will.

You're well equipped for what fight you choose,

You have arms and legs and a brain to use,

And the person who has risen great deeds to do

Began their life with no more than you

YOU are the handicap you must face,

You are the one who must choose your place.

You must say where you want to go,

How much you will study the truth to know;

Spirit has equipped you for life, but He

Let's you decide what you want to be.

Courage must come from the soul within the

Courage must come from the soul within,

The person must furnish the will to win.

So figure it out for yourself, my friend,

You were born with all that the great have had,

With your equipment they all began,

So get hold of yourself and say: "I CAN."

Chapter 2
The Purpose of Life

The purpose of life is to transform or turn our weaknesses and flaws into positive accomplishments or assets that will help us rise to our true state of Divinity to become more like the Spirit. We are descended from Spirit (children of Spirit); however, we need to perfect our soul so that the rough spots in our character are smoothed out. A diamond needs its rough edges smoothed out and polished so that it brilliance can shine, and it is likewise with humans. This is why we need a human body even though it is imperfect and has limitations. The human body is in constant need of repair. Even when you eat right and do everything you possibly can to keep it functioning at its peak, it still ages and takes us through the stages of losing the elasticity of our skin, getting skin pigmentations, losing our youthful figure, wearing eye glasses, hearing loss, stiff joints and all the other factors of maturing. Even with all of the negative aspects of an aging body, we still need a human form to house our soul so that we can ascend. I have come to the conclusion that the human body has a way to turn our arrogant egos into humble lambs.

My mother always said you are once a man or woman and twice a child. Most of us will need some help when we become senior citizens. I always say that we should deposit something into life, with a checking account of love, care and compassion so we will have something to withdraw when we get older and need the care and help of others. We get out of life what we put into it. If we are only concerned about ourselves and our selfish needs and do not reach out to help others, no one will come to help us when we need help. What we give out returns to us. If you give out anger and hate you will receive anger and hate in return.

It is sad that we forget why we came to Earth and what we are here to do. Most of us, me included, wander through life thinking we are here to do one thing and find out much later that we are far off the mark in doing what we agreed to do before we arrived on the planet. Most of us get caught up in dramas, events or activities that satisfy us for a short time. does not serve us in the long run; so we get stuck in a rut, and stop progressing or spiritually moving forward.

These are some truths I have noticed about humans:

1. We are human beings having a spiritual experience.

2. We are human beings with an intellectual mind, and we live in a world that is more intellectual than spiritual, therefore we become like the things we are associated with which is the human mind.

3. The human mind is always busy trying to figure out the logistics of what we should do, when we should do it and how we should do it.

4. This figuring things out causes us to fret and worry about things. The process of analysis of the mind asks, "Is this the right thing to do?"

5. We do not live in a society that is highly spiritual like India is seven days a week.

6. We tend to focus on spirituality, only on Sunday or Saturday if that is your Sabbath.

7. We spend more time fretting, worrying, having anxious thoughts, and feeling conflicted rather than feeling calm and serene.

8. If we could get into and stay in a calm serene state of mind, we would be able to make a deep connection with our Divine self, which is whole, complete and fulfilled.

9. Our Divine self has everything it needs to be whole and complete. It uses other souls and connects with other souls on the planet when it needs to be refreshed or when it needs a tune up or spiritual rejuvenation.

10. Some of us need rejuvenation more frequently to feel whole and complete.

I love to travel and have always traveled, so I tell people and myself that my family is universal. I have met so many beautiful people during my travels. It seems that I adopt someone from wherever I travel. When I traveled to Ghana in 2012, I made a profound statement to the young man and lady I adopted as spiritual children. I was asked by Pasqual if I was afraid that I might die while traveling, and I told him that it did not matter. If I happen to die during my travels, wherever I died they could bury me there, and wherever I was buried was not important to me, because my soul was eternal, and I will live forever through Jesus Christ.

I have grown to have no fear of death. Anyone can quit growing, become complacent, become negative and give up. Living a life that is productive and wholesome and making a difference in life is challenging. We humans have many challenges in life, many we do not seek; however, just as a diamond has to go through its refinement to shine its brightest, we likewise will have our dark nights of the soul. There are some things we choose and have control of, but most of the things that happen to us in life we have little or no control over.

I chose to live in San Diego, without a family. However, there have been many times when I missed not having a family. However, I quickly remind myself of how overprotective my family can be. They want to protect me from experiencing any hurt or pain; however, I have learned a lot from the hardship and emotional and physical pains I have endured. With my family not around to support and lift me up, I have the freedom to take a risk and learn from my mistakes. I learn what to do, what works and what does not work for my spiritual evolution. I learn what to do to avoid feeling alone or lonely. Being and living alone has allowed me to adopt and choose many people as my family members who are not blood relatives, but who treat me like they love me and care about my welfare. I also have learned to develop a special relationship with Jesus, Spirit, the Angelic forces and the Divine life force in the universe that watches over and protects us all.

One thing I have learned about myself is that I like and thrive on relationships. It feeds the gap of not having family, so I tell myself I go to meet my family wherever I go. I have noticed that if anyone is within speaking distance of me, I will start a conversation with them. I love people and I am so happy that Spirit made so many of them for me to interact with and meet. All of this helped me to increase and improve my self-esteem, self-worth and my contribution to the world. Some thoughts to remember about your self-esteem:

Self-Esteem - Although our self-concept has many intricate parts, our self-esteem is composed of many selves. It is your cultural upbringing, your morals and the values of your individual and cultural identities. Your self-esteem tells others how you think and feel about yourself and your relationship to others. Webster's dictionary defines it as "A confidence and satisfaction in oneself." The California State Task Force on Self-Esteem defines self-esteem as "appreciating my own worth, and importance, and having the character to be accountable for myself and to act responsibly towards others." The way you act is a measure of your self-esteem. The four parts of your self-esteem are self-image, self-respect, self-worth and self-confidence.

Self-Esteem - Morals and values of your individual and cultural identities.

A. **Self-Image** – It is the self-projected outside us that shows us the world. The self-image evolves continually, according to the situations and experiences you encounter. Our self-image is fragile and can be distorted, damaged or enhanced. Your environment and the people with whom you associate determine how you see yourself.

B. **Self-Respect** – Is to, like yourself and have a high opinion of yourself as equal to others. If you have little or no respect for the feeling of others, it is because you have been hurt by someone. It is the nature of all human beings to be caring and kind. However, if you have been treated in an unloving, unkind manner, you will become bitter and develop a hard exterior since you are afraid you may get hurt again. One of my mothers' African sayings is "A burnt child fears fire." When unpleasant things happen to us, it makes us afraid to trust for we fear the same thing will happen again.

You must respect yourself enough to want to behave and get along with others. If you are/were in trouble a lot at home, or school, the only image people will have is the bad image you have shown. You can create a new image any time you desire. However, it will require that you change. Most people are too lazy or fear change so they remain the same. We can become comfortable with a bad self-image/concept or a good self-image/concept.

C. **Self-Worth** - Everyone is worthy to be alive. You are worthy to be alive or Spirit would not have created you. If you don't feel worthy, it may be that you are seeing yourself from a distorted negative view that needs updating. No one is all bad. To increase your self-worth, identify positive traits or characteristics that set you apart from others. Ask an elderly person, or anyone who has an unbiased opinion, how they view you. We all do things sometime that makes us feel ashamed. These are some ways you can increase your self-worth and self-esteem:

1. Ask for what you want without creating drama around the asking.
2. Take a risk; step out of your comfort zone and relate in a more genuine way, not as a victim wanting sympathy or pity.
3. Own what you are doing wrong. You are playing the role of a victim because you do not feel you deserve better or this is your role or purpose in life.
4. You learned from your parents how to play the role of victim.
5. You may be unwilling to learn and grow for fear you will lose the people around you.

6. You may play the role of a victim so others can love you, to have a family, to keep a family, to keep a husband, child or lover.
7. You may equate love with abuse and suffering.

D. **Self-Confidence** - Courage, self-assured without fear, willing to take risks. There are five types of persons that tend to destroy our confidence or belief in our self; they are Bullies, Manipulators, Braggers, Critics and Intimidators.

Persons with a high self-esteem know they have a _right to_ the following things:

Place a check mark by the ones you know you deserve.
They have a right to:
___1. Respect
___2. Dignity
___3. Esteem (to be esteemed)
___4. Be appreciated
___5. Empathy (to feel as another feels)
___6. Shared sentiments
___7. Be addressed with kind words
___8. Be given accurate information
___9. Be open; have two-way communication
___10. To have people to give them their full attention
___11. Be cared for
___12. Feel a sense of equality

A Guideline on How to Increase Self-Esteem in Anyone

SAY YES, I CAN
Anonymous

You've all that the greatest of men have had;
Two arms, two hands, two legs, two eyes,

And a brain to us if you would be wise,
With this equipment they all began.
So start from the top and say, "I can."
Look them over, the wise and the great,
They take their food from a common plate,
And similar knives and forks they use,
With similar laces they tie their shoes,
The world considers them brave and smart,
But you've all they had when they made their start.
You can triumph and come to skill,
You can be great if you only will.
You're well equipped for what fight you choose,
You have arms and legs and a brain to use,
And the person who has risen great deeds to do
Began their life with no more than you
YOU are the handicap you must face,

You are the one who must choose your place.
You must say where you want to go,
How much you will study the truth to know;
Spirit has equipped you for life, but He
Let's you decide what you want to be.
Courage must come from the soul within the
Courage must come from the soul within,
The person must furnish the will to win.
So figure it out for yourself, my friend,
You were born with all that the great have had,
With your equipment they all began,
So, get hold of yourself and say: "I CAN.".

1. Specialness - You are special and so is all other life on the planet. Spirit said, "I will make mankind in my image and likeness."

2. Talent - Observe yourself and the children in your life to see their unique talent.

3. Differences - Never envy who another person is, what another does or has. You are not them. Spirit made you different from everyone else.

4. A Gem - Discover the diamond/precious gem inside you; it is there.

5. Weaknesses - Understand and know your weaknesses, and develop them into strengths.

6. Acceptance - Accept who you are, your flaws, imperfections and all. Spirit did not make a mistake; every aspect of you is beautiful to Spirit.

7. Integrity - Be the same all the time; be genuine. No one likes a phony, including you.

8. Character - Develop a strong character foundation, the qualities you would like to see in others: honest dependable.

9. Honesty - Tell the truth, even if it gets you in trouble. It will get you into Heaven, later.

10. Approval - Like and approve the person you see in the mirror each day. If you are doing something wrong stop it.

11. Love - Love and support yourself without being arrogant or feeling superior. You are equal to all people great and small.

12. Value - Accept that you have value in life and are worthy to exist. Spirit gave you life and you are his precious child and creation.

13. Strengths - Find out your special strengths, develop and maximize them.

14. Manners - Have good manners. They are the glue that keeps relationships together. Some important words are: Please, Thank You, I Apologize, Excuse me, May I, Could You, Would You.

15. Interest - Show interest in what others do and they will show interest in what you do.

16. Smile - Smile often. It is good medicine for your soul.

17. Praise - Compliment others. If you can't say something good about yourself or others, keep your mouth shut.

18. Self-Help - What you do to/for others, you do to/for yourself. "What goes around comes around."

19. Appreciation - Appreciate the blessing and gift you are to life.

20. Criticism - Learn to accept more, and criticize or find less fault.

21. Sincerity - Heap large doses of sincere praise on others, and you will be attractive to others.

22. Friend - Be a friend, be friendly and you will have friends.

23. Kind - Be kind to others, if you desire someone to be kind to you. We need all the help we can get.

On Self-Esteem

I am me, in all the world there is no one else like me.
There are persons who have some parts like me, but no one adds up exactly like me.

Therefore, everything that comes out of me is authentically mine because I alone chose it.

I own everything about me.
My body, including everything it does; my mind, including all its thoughts and ideas; my eyes, including the images of all they behold.

My feelings, whatever they may be; Anger, joy, frustration, love, disappointment, excitement

My mouth, and all the words that come out of it polite, sweet or rough, correct or incorrect.

My voice, loud or soft and all my actions whether they are to help others or to help myself.

I own my fantasies, my dreams, my hopes, my fears. I own all my triumphs and successes, all my failures and mistakes.

Because I own all of me, I can become intimately acquainted with me. By so doing I can love me and be friendly with me in all my parts.

I can then make it possible for all of me to work in my best interests. I know there are aspects about myself that puzzle me and other aspects that I do not know.

But as long as I am friendly and loving to myself, I can courageously and hopefully look for the solutions to the puzzles and for ways to find out more about me.

However I look and sound, whatever I say and do, whatever I feel at a given moment in time is me.

This is authentic and represents where I am at the moment in time.

When I review later how I looked and sounded, what I said and did, and how I thought and felt, some parts may turn out to be unfitting. I can discard that, which is unfitting and keep that which proved fitting, and invent something new, for that which I discarded.

I can see, hear, feel, think, say and do. I have the tools to survive, to be close to others, to be productive and to make sense and order out of the world of people and things outside of me.

I own me, and therefore I can engineer me. I am me and I am okay.
Virginia Satir

The Present

The **Present** describes your life: It is a gift and is happening now. I would like to give you some examples of how facts can affect your life and you'll begin to see them as the premises from which all chance of fulfillment grows.

1. No one can bring your life to you.
2. No matter what you do in life, someone important to you isn't going to like it.
3. Though it is painful, rejection won't kill you and it may even lead to growth.
4. Every choice means giving up something else.
5. Some people are not capable of giving you what you are trying to get from them.
6. The way you treat yourself sets the standard for others.
7. There are no quick fixes that can permanently change your life.
8. Life is on a rheostat, not an on and off switch.
9. Some problems cannot be solved, but you can make peace with them.

Excerpted from On A Clear Day You Can See Yourself!
Dr. Sonya Friedman with Guy Kettelhack

Boundaries

Know, practice and learn from your boundaries. Boundaries are dividing lines that separate you from others, or where you end and other people begin. This includes understanding what your limits are, what your needs are and what is unacceptable for you. You can quickly see how your deal-makers and your deal-breakers will help you to define some of your boundaries.

This includes being proactive, or assertive, and asking for what you want. On the other hand, it's also letting petting people know what you don't want or what is unacceptable for you. If you do this you will create your highest self-respect and self-esteem. Do you have boundaries around what you will allow others to say or do to or with you?

Your boundaries are an important yardstick and life compass. You also need to have boundaries that you set with yourself as well as others. What this means is for you to set boundaries between the different parts of your life, for work, relationship and family, so, for example, you don't become a workaholic. You should find or make time for your friends, time to exercise and time to rest and relax. These are some of the ways of you setting boundaries with yourself so you can help you have more balance in your life.

In this day and age there is a big invitation out there to get into a workaholic mode of "Bigger, Better, Faster and more Now." This seems to be the paradigm many people and businesses operate from to the detriment of their soul. It is important to have inner boundaries and to have external boundaries. Together both internal and external boundaries will make a winning combination in your relationships and in your life. We need to find ways to let go to experience more stillness and peace in our mind, body and soul. It is in the stillness of the moment where you will find your greatest strength and peace.

Think Peaceful Thoughts

World Peace
Sustainability
Exploration
Appreciation
Transformation
Organic Living
Expression
Compassion
Consciences
Spirituality
Gratitude
Mind Expansion
Community
Acceptance
Happiness
Love

Weight loss is like a competition,
With ups and downs and all,
And all you have to do to win
Is to rise each time you fall.

Letting Go
Anonymous

LETTING GO does not mean to stop caring; it means not to take responsibility for someone else.

LETTING GO is not to enable others; it is to allow learning from natural consequences.

LETTING GO is to admit my own powerlessness, which means the outcome is not in my hands.

44

LETTING GO is not to try to change or blame others but to make the most of myself.

LETTING GO is not to care for, but to care about.

LETTING GO is not to fix, but to be supportive.

LETTING GO is not to be protective; it's to permit another to face reality.

LETTING GO is not to deny, but to accept.

LETTING GO is not to nag, scold or argue; it is to search out my own shortcomings and correct them.

LETTING GO is not to adjust everything to my desires but to take each day as it comes, and cherish myself in it.

LETTING GO is not to criticize and regulate others but to grow and live for the future.

LETTING GO is to fear less, and love more.

A Negro Speaks of Rivers
Langston Hughes

I've known rivers; I've known rivers
Ancient as the world and older than

The flow of human blood in human veins,
My soul has grown deep like the rivers.

I bathed in the Euphrates, when dawns were young.

45

I built my hut near the Congo, and it lulled me to sleep.

I looked upon the Nile and raised the pyramids above it.

I heard the singing of the Mississippi
When Abe Lincoln went down to New Orleans, and

I've seen its muddy bosom turn all golden in the sunset.
I've known rivers; Ancient, dusky rivers.
My soul has grown deep like the rivers.

Prayer of St. Francis of Assisi

Lord, make me an instrument of your peace.
Where there is hatred, let me sow love;
Where there is injury, pardon;
Where there is doubt, faith;
Where there is despair, hope;
Where there is darkness, light;
Where there is sadness, joy.

O Divine Master, Grant that
I may not so much seek to be consoled as to console;
To be understood as to understand;
To be loved as to love;
For it is in giving that we receive;
It is in pardoning that we are pardoned;
It is in dying that we area born to eternal life

Don't Walk in Front of Me – I May Not Follow.
Don't Walk Behind Me - I May Not Lead.
Walk Beside Me – and Just Be My Friend.

Descriptive Words to Heal the Anxious Spirit

Describe a time when you felt each of the emotions listed below.

1. I felt FRUSTRATED when

2. I felt LONELY when

3. I felt EXCITED when

4. I felt ANGRY when

5. I felt AFRAID when

6. I felt RESENTFUL when

7. I felt SORRY when

8. I felt DISCOURAGED when

9. I felt JOYFUL when

10. I felt THANKFUL when

Make up some sentences of your own below, using other emotions.

I felt _____

when_____

Chapter 3
The Road Less Traveled

The road that we travel less in life is the road of seeing ourselves as an extension or a child of the Divine who I call Spirit. If we could stay in that role for one hour a day, we would see ourselves as unlimited in our ability to manifest anything we desire like perfect health, career, perfect love, relationships, abundance, prosperity, harmony and peace without conflict, tension, anxiety or stress. I have found for myself, it is challenging to be in that state 100 percent for 15 minutes unless I am in a meditative state. Our mind is so busy; it is always responding to everything in our outer world that it sees or comes into contact with. In addition, we have a million or more thoughts a minute flashing through our brain, and since we like the stimulation, we let our mind wander in and out of states of awareness that may or may not be in our highest good. I have been widowed and divorced. I have been single for a while, and I feel no need at the present to be in a relationship. I am finding that when I am alone or single I am more open to reach out to other people.

When I was married, my focus was on family and not on connecting with other people. I was very limited and myopic about relationships, because my energy was focused on perfecting the relationship I had. It takes time, energy, passion, love, taking care of, emotionally feeding and commitment to sustain a relationship.

Now that I am single, my attitude is that I go to meet my family or my friends whoever or wherever they are. I am a more open and fun person to be around now. This has opened me up to a new mindset. I truly believe that some of us come into the world to be alone, some find their soul mate, some of us come to be a part of the family of mankind and some people are here to learn How to Be Alone Without Being/Feeling Lonely.

Living alone can allow us the opportunity to understand our greatness and who we are as a person. Greatness is a natural state anyone can enter into. This state or feeling of greatness can give us a lifetime of achievement and peace. We are all at a certain level of greatness already in our life.

There is greatness in all of us; it is an inner process. We are quick to point out the faults or weaknesses in ourselves and others, but fail to point out our greatness. Our greatness may be sleeping inside of us and we may need to uncover our potential. Look for how you can be great without focusing on the ego or self. Some things that can blind us to our greatness are:

1. Having a sense of false modesty or a sense of being inadequate or flawed in some way.

2. Confusion about how to be great; our legacy is a by-product of our greatness.

3. Family expectations that you be "normal" rather than be great.

4. How do you want to show up in the world?

5. Do you have a belief about creating value for yourself?

If so, what is it? Write your answer below.

6. What can you do to create value for yourself?

7. Others are watching you; how can you create value for others through the way you live your life?

Judge Less of Ourselves and Others

How authentic are we when we spend so much time in judgment? Being in judgment reduces our ability to be open. When we are open we can see possibilities and draw them to us. When we are in judgment we cannot see beyond what we judge. When we are open we can welcome authenticity. When we are in judgment it is difficult to see what is real and what is not.

I prefer an open world that authentically includes everyone, and where even when we judge ourselves, it is done in the spirit of possibilities. Who are we to judge others? Whether we are judging their sexual preference or what they wore today, who are we to judge? Unless you have walked in the shoes of the person you are judging, you have no real knowledge of what they are going through. One thing is pretty clear— if you are alive on this planet there is some issue you are dealing with, have dealt with or are beginning to deal with. We each have stuff that clouds our perspective and can make life challenging. And unless you know the depth of stuff that someone else is handling, how can you judge their behavior or their decisions?

If you are one who lives in judgment I offer you the opportunity to live a more open life. Let go of all the "should" thoughts that you have. This will help you to adjust your judgment of people and things. If you are already an open person I applaud you. Continue to be a role model for authenticity. "The choice is yours," says Norma Hollis.

One of the purposes of life is for us to be a good earth parent for Spirit's children. Many of us do not realize that the role of a parent is a sacred and holy role. The reason we do not know or understand is because for us to become parents we have to engage in a joyous, fun, loving activity called sexual intercourse. Many of us think it is just for us to enjoy ourselves. Very few of us enter sexual intercourse as an opportunity to change the destiny of a child's life, or to chart the course of history in a new direction with the sex partner we are with.

Many babies who are born are an accident and the result of passionate love making between two people. Some are born to give pleasure to the parent. Some are born because a man, woman or both feel unfulfilled or incomplete. While many people who give birth to babies do so unconsciously and have no plans for how they will help the child be a masterpiece to humanity or help the child find their right their right path in life to develop their gifts and talents, there are a small minority who are enlightened and see the gift children bring. Most of what is done with children is to show them how to be a duplicate of the imperfections and flaws of their parents who realize who they are. Yet they fail to realize that who they are is Spirit's gift to them, and what they make of their lives is their gift to Spirit. They do not realize that they are created in the images and likeness of Spirit and came to earth to do great things. I do believe that Spirit allows us to pick our parents before we come to earth, and it seems some of us make a bad choice of the persons we pick as parents. Some of the parents we select can cause us to have a short life span through their use of drugs, their selfish habits or reckless lifestyle.

I am glad I chose the parents I did. I chose a mother who only had a third grade education, who worked two jobs to provide us the bare necessities of life, who was fearful, who felt unloved by her mother and who was creative. She sewed our clothes, made fruit preserves, kept a vegetable garden and bought and kept chickens for us to take care of and to give us eggs to eat for lunch. I chose a mom who had a passion for education because she was denied that opportunity. She could not go to school because she had to work in the cotton field in Alabama to help her family survive. I had a mom who said to me, it seemed ever day of my life, "Get an education. I want one of my children to get an education." I had a mom who knew that she was beautiful. I would watch her as she looked in the mirror and said to herself, "I am a beautiful woman." I chose a mom who drank alcohol with my dad, who had many fights with him as a result of their weekend drinking and who later became an alcoholic and did not quit drinking alcohol until she was 67.

I chose a dad who was smart. He felt that he was the smartest man in the world and said there was no college for him to attend when he graduated from high school, so he went through the 12th grade two times. I chose a dad who was witty, humorous, had the gift of gab, was creative, was a risk taker, unafraid, drank alcohol and physically abused my mom when they were drinking together. He encouraged me to stand up for myself, never said "no" to me, felt I could accomplish anything, paid me $1 whenever I got an "A" and always wanted the best for me. My grandmother on my mom's side complained about my dad, because she said he felt the sun rose and set in me.

It is said I looked like my dad's mom, who died when he was 12. I chose a dad who felt that I was the best, should be number one and who was disappointed because I was voted the vice president in school instead of president. I was okay with being the vice president, as I had less responsibility. I had a dad who loved smoking Camel cigarettes which caused him to get emphysema, problems with breathing and eventually contributed to his death. My dad's biggest weakness was that he loved women and drinking. It was this deadly combination that caused him to have a car accident and become physically impaired where he no longer wanted to live because of the pain he had to endure from his hip fracture. My dad and I were very close. He once drove from Pensacola Florida to San Diego California to get my permission for him to die. Naturally I did not give my permission, but he died anyway at 60 of a heart attack due to his use of tobacco.

I chose to have parents who had many flaws, but who managed to put my needs before their needs. A good enough parent is all you need to help you succeed in life. Are you a good enough parent?

Good Parenting: A New Look at Old Behavior
Parenting Traits and Qualities

Much of the time a good enough parent:
- ☐ Is nurturing
- ☐ Is flexible

- ☐ Is understanding
- ☐ Is consistent
- ☐ Allows growth
- ☐ Acknowledges, the child as a unique individual,
- ☐ Provide the basics and a positive emotional atmosphere (protection, safety, security, food, shelter)

Key words for a good enough parent include:
- ☐ Attention
- ☐ Involvement
- ☐ Guidance
- ☐ Communication
- ☐ Comfort
- ☐ Validation
- ☐ Flexibility
- ☐ Understanding
- ☐ Education
- ☐ Cooperation
- ☐ Listens without judgment
- ☐ Is accepting
- ☐ Provides direction and age-appropriate guidance
- ☐ Knows how to let go (is not possessive)
- ☐ Establishes and maintains rituals
- ☐ Is an ally
- ☐ Is a role model, models wholeness, balance
- ☐ Touch
- ☐ Consistency
- ☐ Structure
- ☐ Positive reinforcement
- ☐ Confidence building
- ☐ Age-appropriate expectations
- ☐ Love
- ☐ Good coping skills
- ☐ Hopefulness
- ☐ Trust (opportunities to ear

A Good Enough Parent Avoids Making a Child Feel "Not Okay":

☐   Has or enforces a reasonable number of procedures and rules

☐   Much of the time is not "too busy" to pay attention to the child

☐   Speaks with the child without anger or irritation much of the time

The Road Less Traveled is the Road To Be Loved

Love is the answer to every problem you will encounter in life. The law of Spirit is perfect, and the law of the Lord is perfect because it is love. You are made perfect in the law when you enter into conscious communion with love. Love is the fulfillment of the law of Spirit; that is, it is only through love, the law of Spirit, that love can fulfill itself in your experience, because love harmonizes everything and unifies everything. Love gives to everything, flows through everything and is everything. Love does not require you to be anything or do anything. It only requires that you give of your best self to the universe to serve mankind. So you can never make the most perfect use of the law of your life unless that use is motivated by love. Because who you are is Spirit's gift to you, and what you make of your life is your gift to Spirit. We all seek and want love, however few of us know how to get the love we need and crave.

Most of us look outside ourselves for love. However, love begins with accepting who you are with all your flaws, shortcomings and imperfections. Charles Bukowski says it is possible to love a human if you don't know them too well. Are you able to see the beauty inside yourself in spite of your human flaws or lack of perfection? Sophia Loren says nothing makes a woman more beautiful than the belief that she is beautiful. It may be that we are too harsh and critical of ourselves and others. Oscar Wilde says that if you want to tell people the truth, make them laugh first, otherwise they will kill you. It could be that we need to learn how to laugh at ourselves. It may be that we take ourselves and life too seriously.

Laughter is the oil that the keeps the machinery of our mind, body and soul running. The key is to have a constant dialogue with yourself to see where in your life and how you can become better. According to Plato wise men talk because they have something to say, and fools talk because they have to say something. We need to learn how to use the gift of silence. It is true that there is a time for everything: there is a time to speak and a time to be still. It is in the stillness and silence of the moment that we hear the inner voice of the Divine Spirit.

As the artist weds himself to beauty, imbibing the essence or spirit of beauty that it may be transmitted to the canvas or awaken to cold marble to living form, so you must wed yourself to love. You must imbibe its spirit. Love is more than a sentiment. It is a deep sense of the underlying unity and beauty of all life, the goodness running through everything, the givingness of life to everything.

Affirm Today and Say:

Today I bestow the essence of Love upon everything.

Everyone and everything is lovely to me.

My soul meets the soul of the universe in everyone.

Everything is beautiful, everything is meaningful.

This love is a healing power touching everything into wholeness, healing the wounds of experience with its divine balm. I know that this love essence is the very substance of life, the creative principle in back of everything, flowing through my whole being—spiritual, emotional, mental and physical.

It flows in transcendent loveliness into my world of thought and form, ever renewing and vitalizing, bringing joy, harmony and blessing to everything and everyone it touches.

You are to know that good keeps you in perfect activity, surrounds you with love and friendship and brings the experience of joy to everything you do.

Another Road Less Traveled is the Road to Greatness

Greatness is a mindset of excellence. We have an inner power that makes us calm, serene and peaceful. You have feelings and can create an attitude of abundance and prosperity through your imagination and beliefs. With practice you are able to manifest anything you desire in an instant. When you are operating from greatness everything you engage in is about excellence. There is no discord or confusion in your life. The thing that will keep you anchored is your inner state of knowing who you are and what you know with certainty you can do.

Another Road Less Traveled is the Road of Wealth

I am becoming more comfortable with the idea of having lots of money. My fear around money is decreasing. All of this will allow me the freedom around money. I need to see myself with money before I actually obtain it. I am now developing a "gardening millionaire mindset" to create the soil and environment for me create what I plan to do and how I plan to go about creating the million dollars I want to acquire and have, before I share my money with the family of mankind. This is a big new game for me that was scary at first, but is becoming more comfortable the more I think about becoming a millionaire. I have had a poverty mindset for a long time. I am becoming excited about having money to "spare and share" so that I support the three orphanages I have chosen in Africa.

I never considered what a winnable game for my business would look like. Now I realize that the thing I have been avoiding most of my life is to have a lot of money and be a millionaire. I cannot give money to the children in Africa unless I am willing to do what it takes to create the money I want to give. Coaching is one of the income streams I have chosen to help me generate the money to become a wealthy philanthropist to give to my charitable causes for children in Africa, and I am committed to make it happen.

Another Road Less Traveled is the Road of Joy and Happiness

We are motivated by pain or pleasure. We are always moving toward pleasure or away from pain. I have decided to have more pleasure in my life. What do you choose?

Take a few moments now and write about what you have chosen in the past that has not served you and what you are willing to do in the future to change this pattern. This could very well be the healing on your path to be whole so that you no longer feel alone or lonely.

7 Keys To Happiness

I read the current scientific studies on happiness and came up with 7 points. Each of them can help lift your mood and give you a sense of accomplishment. I wanted to share them with you, so you can try them out for yourself. The idea is to try to do as many of them as you can in an hour.

1. Boost your energy by getting up and moving around.

2. Taking a brisk 10-minute walk is best, because when you are moving faster, your metabolism speeds up and the activity is good for your focus and mood and helps you retain information.

3. Reach out to friends. Arrange a lunch date or send an email to someone you haven't seen for a while. Socializing boosts moods and having close bonds with others is one of the keys to happiness.

4. Get an old task out of the way. If you've been procrastinating about a chore, tackle it now. Like making that doctor or dental appointment, or arranging to get broken equipment fixed. You'll feel a sense of relief and a burst of energy.

5. Create a calmer environment. Just clearing some space around you or getting things in order will give you a sense of serenity.

6. Plan some future fun. Decide to get to that new movie, order a book you have been planning to read or plan an activity with friends or family. Having fun on a regular basis is necessary to happiness, and anticipation is a part of that.

7. Do a good deed. Something as simple as holding a door for someone or offering praise can help, because the adage "do good, feel good" really works.

Act happy. Smile! Just going through the motion of happiness lifts your spirits and makes you more approachable.

Another Road Less Traveled is Giving Up the Need to Be Perfect

I had a coaching session with a coaching partner. After one my coaching sessions I felt hurt by the words someone I admired and respected said to me about my coaching session with her. I asked for her feedback about how she felt about my coaching session with her. She stated that I should not do traditional coaching and that she would not hire me as a coach. I took her words to heart and I felt hurt, because I had recently decided I wanted to use coaching as a second stream of income. Now I was hearing someone tell me this was not a good idea and that it would not work for me. My coach partner reminded me that everyone can get better at what they do and that I deserved a second chance.

After much reflection I realized what I had done wrong and called the person to make a correction. I suddenly realized the person I coached had her own coaching program, and I was coaching her on a coaching method using the Coachville "PlayTwoWin" Coaching method. I also followed the script from the book (which I never do) because I wanted to introduce her to the new technique I was learning. I made several mistakes. One was I should have used her coaching program process and material, her authenticity grid, to coach her. I am highly intuitive. I felt some resistance to what I was doing with my client but ignored my intuition because I wanted to complete the project, which was not a good idea. I did not figure it out until later that I had not developed the necessary rapport with her before I started talking to her.

Rapport building is very important. It acknowledges the person's humanity as being a worthwhile person. I knew this, but just like you I sometimes get up into the logistics of things and forget that I have a caring, wise and intelligent person in front of me. Acknowledgement is very important to us all. I called the person I coached to see if she would be willing to allow me to coach her again, using her coaching model. She said yes. I realized that my need to be perfect prompted me to read from a script which seemed stiff and rigid to her. I will never do that again. Life is a series of taking corrective actions to help us accomplish our goals. It is a trial and error process. Sometimes we are perfect, and other times we are way off track. It is okay for you and me to be imperfect and to make mistakes. We learn from our trials and errors. We do not need to be perfect or do things right all the time. I suggest you give up your need to be perfect or to have certainty. This is a sure recipe to create undue stress in your life which you do not need.

I have a better understanding of what it means to respect and acknowledge the humanity of the other person we are speaking to or with. If we want to receive acknowledgement from someone, we must give it first. We must give respect in order to receive respect. People will say hurtful things to us if they feel they have not been acknowledged by us. I missed an opportunity to brag to her about her great coaching program.

Instead, I introduced her to a new coaching program that she knew nothing about without saying how wonderful her coaching program was. This was a great life lesson. The universe will give us immediate feedback about what we are giving out. People will give back to us based on what they feel they have received, be it bad, indifferent or good.

I am reminded that what I interpreted from this person as criticism was a statement by the other person saying, "I am here and want to be recognized and acknowledged." Her nonverbal message to me was "my coaching program is just as important as the one you are bragging about." When information or feedback is given in a manner that does not elevate or support the person with whom we are interacting, the response we get back from them can seem like criticism, or feel unloving. We all need to be accepted and appreciated, because it is the lubrication that oils the inner dialogue between people. We all need to get and stay in our heart space before we start a conversation with another person. If feedback it is not given in a framework of compassion and love, it will be received and interpreted as negative by the other person. I have decided that I will be proactive when I am interacting with others and not take everything people say to me as personal. We can all hear what is being said to us as positive or negative. We should never let the words anyone says to us decide what we should do, who we should become or how we should live our life.

Even though I have not made much money in my coaching business, I am going to keep at it until I get better with my connection skills and increase my wealth self-image. As we develop and grow as an individual and business person so will our attraction factor increase so that we attract the people who are worthy and deserving of us and who are willing to pay us what we want and deserve. We sometimes need to look at what we are grateful for in our life. I had to remind myself that I had been hired by someone earlier in the year who gave me $350 for a one-hour coaching session. That reflection on my gratitude helped me to snap out of my depressive state. I now accept that I will continue to look for ways to improve my coaching skills and coaching practice. I will persist at coaching until I have a thriving $20,000 a month coaching business. I will not let anyone decide what I should or should not do, and you should do the same. I am choosing to say goodbye to my smallness and hello to my greatness. I accept that I do not need to be perfect to do anything. I just need to be happy and enjoy myself and I claim the same for you.

Another Road Less Traveled is the Road to Beauty

There is an obsession in America with beauty. Beauty is an idea or concept that beauty is eternal and that we will never age. Women spend billions of dollars on trying to maintain their beauty with products and plastic surgery to no avail. We do age and we eventually have to come to grips with the fact that there is no fountain of youth. Beauty is an elixir and a power that we worship in our society. Don Miguel Ruiz states that women say, "Oh my Spirit, my beauty is going away. Will my man still love me if I am not as attractive? Now he will see other women who are more attractive than me." None of us want to age, however we have to accept the fact that our body does and will age.

Another Road Less Traveled is the Road of Aging

We are caught up in our quest to be eternally young. Age is physical, mental and Spiritual. At the age of 90, Charles Fillmore affirmed daily, "I fairly sizzle with zeal and enthusiasm, as I spring forth with a mighty zeal to do the things that can only be done by me." We are too consumed. Don Miguel Ruiz says we resist aging. We believe that because someone is old, it means she is not beautiful. "This belief is completely wrong. If you see a newborn baby, it is beautiful. Well, an old person is also beautiful. The problem is the emotion we have in our eyes to perceive what is and what is not beautiful. We have all these judgments, all these programs that put limits on our own happiness that push us to self-rejection and to reject other people also."

Another Road Less Traveled is the Road of Freedom

The French novelist and philosopher Albert Camus wrote that freedom is nothing but a chance to be better, to learn more, love more and experience more. We have the freedom to make different choices, to seek greater meaning and fulfillment. Our freedom does not depend on our outer conditions; it is inside us. We are free to choose fear or faith, criticism or support, to be a victim or be victorious. We are free to be our best self and to live from that space. We are free to see, to feel, to smell, to eat or not eat; we are free to think what thoughts we will allow and which beliefs we accept as our own. We are free to be ourselves and to not be an imitation of another person.

Another Road Less Traveled is the Road of Peace

The road to peace is to let go of the envy, resentment, jealousy, hate and anger we are holding toward another person. When we are ready to travel the road to peace, we have to forgive everything and everyone we feel has harmed or hurt us, real or imagined. Use this affirmation on a daily basis to help you feel more peace in your heart and in your life.

I Am Willing to Forgive and Be Forgiven

Willingness is the key that unlocks the door to forgiveness. I now declare that I am willing to forgive and to be forgiven.

The power of this declaration begins its good work within me, and I release all thoughts of ill will and all feelings of resentment toward myself and others.

I am willing to cooperate with the forgiving love of Universal Mind and allow it to heal any inharmonious thoughts, feelings or relationships.

I forgive myself and others. I willingly release the excess baggage of unforgiveness, the heaviness of guilt, the burden of judgment, doubt, the hurtful thoughts of self-pity, misunderstanding and the pain over my actions or the actions of others.

All these I willingly release to Universal Mind's redeeming love for cleansing, healing and transforming.

As I willingly give and receive forgiveness, I am filled with love, joy, understanding, peace and harmony.

Another Road Less Traveled is Facing Our Immortality, Death

I attended the stage production of the Pulitzer award play, WIT last night. It was about how a college professor dealt with ovarian cancer and all of the things she encountered in her medical treatment for cancer. Death catches most of us by surprise, and when it does we are not prepared to die or want to die. None of us get out of life alive, and no one has found a way to live forever whether you are a Christian, Muslim, Atheist or Agnostic. It does not matter whether you believe in Spirit or not—we all die. No one gets out life of alive, and no one lives forever. My belief is that our body was given to us by Spirit so that our soul could evolve and be refined. Both our body and our soul belong to Spirit. We were made by Spirit, and have been given dominion over the earth. We are a little lower than the Angels, and we are here on planet earth to evolve, grow and develop our soul. Watching the play allowed me to affirm my belief in my relationship with Spirit. I found myself talking to Spirit and saying many things like: I do not want to have cancer, I do not want to be sick like this, I do not want to take medication, I do not want to be in pain when I die. I want to die in ease, grace, peace   and lovingly make my exit from earth.

The Serenity Prayer

Spirit, grant me the serenity to accept the things I cannot change;
Courage to change the things I can and the wisdom to know the difference.
Living one day at a time; Enjoying one moment at a time and
Accepting change as the pathway to peace

The Footprints in the Sand
Mary Stevenson

One night I had a dream...

I dreamed I was walking along the beach with the Lord, and across the sky flashed scenes from my life. For each scene I noticed two sets of footprints in the sand;

One belonged to me, and the other to the Spirit.

When the last scene of my life flashed before us, I looked back at the footprints in the sand. I noticed that many times along the path of my life,

There was only one set of footprints.

I also noticed that it happened at the very lowest and saddest times in my life. This really bothered me, and I questioned the Lord about it. "Lord, you said that once I decided to follow you, you would walk with me all the way;

But I have noticed that during the most troublesome times in my life,

There is only one set of footprints.

I don't understand why in times when I needed you the most, you should leave me."

The Lord replied, "My precious, precious child. I love you, and I would never, never leave you during your times of trial and suffering.

When you saw only one set of footprints, It was then that I carried you."

Our Thoughts Are Prayers

Our thoughts are prayers
And we are always praying
Our thoughts are prayers,
So be careful of what you are saying
Seek a higher consciousness
A state of peacefulness
Know that Spirit is always there, everywhere
So every thought you think is a prayer and is answered.

Angels on the Wing

When you feel abandoned from life's every good thing,
Remember the comfort brought to us by angels on the wing.

The Invitation
Oriah Mountain Dreamer, Indian Elder, May 1994

It doesn't interest me what you do for a living, I want to know what you ache for, and if you dare to dream of meeting your heart's longing.

It doesn't interest me how old you are. I want to know if you will risk looking like a fool for the love of your dreams, and for the adventure of being alive.

It doesn't interest me what planets are squaring your moon, I want to know if you have touched the center of your own sorrow, if you have been opened by life's betrayals or have become shriveled and closed from fear of further pain.

I want to know if you can sit with pain, mine or your own, without moving to hide or fake it or fix it.

I want to know if you can be with joy, mine or your own; if you can dance with wildness and let ecstasy fill you to the tips of your fingers and toes without cautioning to be careful, be realistic, or to remember the limitations of being human.

It doesn't interest me if the story you're telling me is true. I want to know if you can disappoint another to be true to yourself, if you can bear the accusation of betrayal and not betray your own Soul.

65

I want to know if you can see beauty, even if it's not pretty every day, and if you can source your life from Spirit's presence.

I want to know if you can live with failure, yours and mine, and still stand on the edge of a lake and shout to the silver of the full moon, "YES!"

It doesn't interest me to know where you live or how much money you have. I want to know if you can get up after a night of grief and despair, wary and bruised to the bone, and do what needs to be done for the children.

It doesn't interest me who you are, how you came to be here. I want to know if you will stand in the center of the fire with me and not shrink back.

It doesn't interest me where or what or with whom you have studied. I want to know what sustains you from the inside when all else falls away.

I want to know if you can be alone with yourself, and if you truly like the company you keep in the empty moments.

12 Steps To Having Absolutely No Problems In Your Life
Thomas J. Leonard, A Perfect Life Program

1. Change your sources of energy. The friction that comes from problems is energizing you, albeit expensively.

2. Hang out exclusively with people who have zero problems. This may require a new rolodex.

3. Eliminate tolerations in all their forms. Tolerations are the breeding ground of problems.

4. Simplify your life. A complicated life is a request for problems.

5. Adopt a more advanced personal operating system. Yours is probably buggy, so upgrade.

6. Perfect your personal foundation. When boundaries are strong and standards are high, problems disappear.

7. Fully embrace integrity. Integrity is that which affords flourishment.

8. Automate everything that is automate-able and more: Bill paying reminders, paperwork, administrivia

9. Have healthy reserves in all areas: time, love, money, space, opportunities, and solutions.

10. Declare yourself to be a "problem-free zone." Tell yourself. Tell the world.

11. Take the path of least resistance. There is always an easier—and probably—better way.

12. Abandon all hope. Hope is what you cling to when you think you can overcome yourself.

Thoughts to Live By: The Journey of Life
Ida Greene RN, MFCC, Ph.D.

Maybe, Spirit wanted us to meet the wrong people before meeting the right one, so that when we finally meet the right person we will know how to be grateful for that special gift.

Maybe, when the door of happiness closes, another opens, but oftentimes we look so long at the closed door that we don't see the one which has opened for us.

Maybe, the best kind of friend is the kind you can sit on a porch and swing with, never say a word and then walk away feeling like it was the best conversation you've ever had.

Maybe, it is true that we don't know what we've got until we lose it, but it is also true that we don't know what we have been missing until it arrives.

Giving someone all your love is never an assurance that they will love you back! Don't expect love in return; just wait for it to grow in their heart, but if it does not, be content it grew in yours.

It only takes a minute to get a crush on someone, an hour to like someone and a day to love someone, but it takes a lifetime to forget someone.

Don't go for looks; they can deceive. Don't go for wealth, even that fades away. Go for someone who makes you smile, because it only takes a smile to make a dark day bright. Find the one who makes your heart smile.

There are moments in life when you may miss someone so much that you just want to pick them from your dreams and hug them for real.

LOVE
Anonymous

Love may sometimes be a light thing
You may wear it like a flower; or a ring upon your finger.
Yet love has lasting power.
But whether love lights lightly, or for eternity,
You find the more it binds you,
The more it sets you free.
Love may sometimes lay a heavy load
You think you cannot bear,
But love and you together, have strength enough to spare.
Love lifts you on invisible

But ah, what mighty wings!

When life is dearest and most blessed,

Love is the song it sings.

An Inventory to Assess Your Strengths

1. **This Inventory Does Not:**
  A. Measure intelligence

  B. Measure mental health

  C. Give rights or wrongs

2. **What It Does:**
  A. Increases understanding of your style and the strengths of others

  B. Provides guidelines for increasing your effectiveness

3. **It Assumes:**
A. All people have styles of behavior and personality

B. All styles have strengths

C. Weaknesses are often strengths taken to an excess or overused

D. Behavioral styles may change under stress

E. We need all types

F. Behavioral styles impact group efficiency, effectiveness, innovation and creativity

4. **The Three Behavioral Styles Are**:
  A. **Altruistic - Nurturing**

  B. **Analytic - Autonomizing (academic/autocratic behaviors)**

  C. **Assertive - Directive**

Altruistic - Nurturing Type

Altruistic – Nurturing types of people feel best about what they are doing. They enjoy being helpful in some way to others who can genuinely benefit from their help. These folks feel most rewarded by others_when they are treated as a warm and friendly person who wants to be of help and who is deserving of thanks and appreciation for giving help. They feel distant from and somewhat contemptuous of people who constantly compete with and try to take advantage of others or who are cold and unresponsive to gestures of friendliness.

The following are Strengths and Weakness of:
  Altruistic – Nurturing People:
  Strengths ------------>Weaknesses

Trusting	Gullible
Idealistic	Wishful
Modest	Self-Effacing
Caring	Smothering
Accepting	Passive
Optimistic	Impractical
Helpful	Self-Denying
Devoted	Self-Sacrificing
Supportive	Submissive

Assertive - Directing People
Strengths ------------> Weaknesses

Self-Confident	Arrogant
Enterprising	Opportunistic
Ambitious	Ruthless
Organizer	Controlling
Persuasive	Pressuring
Forceful	Dictatorial
Quick to Act	Rash
Competitive	Combative
Risk-taker	Gambler

Adapted from the Strength Deployment Inventory

The New Road to Travel to Feel Less Alone or Lonely

Never talk defeat. Use words like hope, belief, faith, victory.

Life's blows cannot break a person whose spirit is warmed at the fire of enthusiasm.

It is of practical value to learn to like you. Since you must spend so much time with yourself you might as well get some satisfaction out of the relationship.

Develop a tremendous faith in Spirit and that will give you a humble yet soundly realistic faith in yourself.

Miracles come in all sizes. If you start believing in little miracles, then you can work your way up to bigger miracles.

Love
1 Cor. 13, 4-7

Love is Patient and Kind;
Love is Not Jealous or Conceited;
Love is Not Proud or Selfish;
Love is Not Ill-Mannered;
Love is Not Irritable;
Love Does Not Hold a Grudge;
Love is Not Happy With Evil;
Love is Happy With the Truth;
Love Never Gives Up;
Its Faith, Hope and Patience Never Fail

Chapter 4
How To Be Alone Without Feeling Lonely

I believe in love, I believe in romance, and I believe in marriage. I was married two times; widowed once and divorced once. I felt alone when I was widowed and felt odd after my divorce. My married friends did not know how to relate to me. I felt they were uneasy and fearful that I might get interested in their spouse. I was in a domestic violent marriage, which they were unaware of and I needed time alone to heal. My ex-husband instilled fear in me that if I got into a relationship with another man he would kill me, so I stayed to myself and this was the start of my being single for 30 years. This was really a time where I grew into my own power and discovered who I was, what I had to offer to the world, what my purpose was for being born and how I could partner with Spirit to use my gifts in a larger way.

When I was a young child I felt that Spirit wanted to use me in a larger way. I felt it had something to do with religion, because I surrendered my life to Jesus at the age of 6. I thought I might marry a minister or something along those lines. My second husband was the son of a minister, but he was far from being a holy man. He was plagued with many demons. As I later found out and the reason for my divorce, he was an alcoholic, went to prison for stealing social security checks and raping someone, and he beat his wife before me. I did not know any of this until he started having relations with another woman, and I decided to leave him.

This is when his abuse of me started. However, after much physical abuse, hurt, pain and confusion I did divorce my husband. This was the beginning of my spiritual journey into me finding who I was, why I was kept alive and to discover what I was to do with my life. Both my husband and I were into Amway, a network marketing business which I wanted to grow and expand. A friend told me about a religion called Religious Science that helped people become successful. Terri Cole Whittaker, a minister of this religion, was having a Winner's Circle Breakfast every Tuesday, and I started attending the breakfast and the church. I heard Mark Victor Hansen speak on love and many other New Thought leaders in this movement, including Reverend Bobbie Spires and Reverend Robert Rankin who was teaching a ministerial class at East West University in Long Beach California. I took the class and received a Doctorate in Divinity and a PhD in Theology, with a minor in Psychology using my Master's degree in Counseling from San Diego State University.

I still needed healing of my self-esteem from the emotional abuse of domestic violence, so I started teaching classes on self-esteem, wrote two healing books, *How to Improve Self-Esteem in the African-American Child* and *Self-Esteem, the Essence of You.* I conducted self-esteem classes, domestic violence and anger management groups in all of the women shelters in San Diego and started teaching my own classes for women. My passion was to end the violence and abuse of women. I discovered that it was easier for children to end abusive relationships than adults, so I started teaching a Self-Esteem Rites of Passage class and Anger Management classes for children. I later modified the classes and added Etiquette classes, a Self-Esteem Pageant, Anger Management for children and a Leave a Legacy Awards Luncheon for Adults. Today I am only doing an annual Self-Esteem, Etiquette and Anger Management class for children.

I do feel that our ability to live or be alone has a lot to do with our level of self-esteem and self-worth. A positive self-concept enables you to accept yourself, in spite of shortcomings or perceived deficiencies. If you acknowledge yourself as a work of fine art, a masterpiece evolving, you accept yourself as you are, with the capacity to improve and become better. Be aware that your self-concept is not one but two-dimensional. Our self-concept is greatly influenced by what we think, how we feel and how we act. You have a personal self-concept identity and a spiritual self-concept identity. Your self-image (inner self-picture) is formed based on the concept you have of yourself.

Your identity is the core aspect of you. I refer to it as self-concept because there are no two people alike. Spirit created everyone different and unique. Therefore, you are special, one of a kind. You are as different from everyone else in the universe as an apple is from an orange. There is no comparison between the two. Spirit has built within each person a spiritual yardstick to which we all must grow before we die. Each lesson is equally challenging and hard for each person. We decide with Spirit, before we come to earth, the best conditions (parents, race, sex, country) to help us grow and blossom spiritually. The human experience is a refining process necessary for our soul to evolve and develop.

Spirit allows us to decide the particulars of how we want to live our life and what we want to do or accomplish. Some of us decide to come to earth to give joy to our parents for a day, a year, 7 years or 70 years. Whatever we do with our life, it must be a masterpiece for Spirit to behold. From Spirit we come and to Spirit we return after our brief journey on earth. And since no one knows when the final hour will be to return to Spirit, it is best that we make each day count. You must do your best daily to be the best person you can be. Sometimes you do not get a second chance to clear up a destructive or unproductive life. It is easy to look at another person and wish you were them. Yet, you do not know the painful trials they endure as they smile. Remember, you chose this lifetime. You said yes to Spirit and to your life circumstances. Spirit never promised any of us that we would live a life free of hardship or challenge.

Life is an unpainted canvas. You can create as many scenes as you like. Life is a journey, not a destination. When you stop growing, you slowly die. So pause if you must. Take time to enjoy the scenery and the stage production you created. For what you are is Spirit's gift to you. What you make of yourself is your gift to Spirit. When you die and leave the planet, will you leave Spirit a masterpiece of your life experiences or give back the heap of ashes from whence you came? Who you are is beautiful and magnificent. You are one of a kind, a rare gem.

Your self-concept is the basic foundation of who you are. To be fully the person Spirit designed requires that you develop both your personal and spiritual self-concept. Most of us spend little time on developing our spiritual self-concept. It is just as important as your personal self-concept. Both aspects of your nature need to be cultivated and developed. Our other basic human needs are support, desire and self-esteem.

Support - Mental, Physical, Emotional Body - We

achieve maturity and grow spiritually by working on our mental, physical and emotional bodies. We have an inner drive to achieve, excel and be a better person to gain mastery over our lower nature to become the Christ within. We have been given a physical body to work through our imperfections, our negative emotions and thoughts of self-doubt. Your goal is to seek ways to improve these three aspects of yourself. This provides the self-discipline you need to complete your primary goal of soul perfection.

Desire - Dream/Goals - Believe in yourself and know you are valuable to life. Like yourself enough to have goals. Be willing to take risks or plan how you will live your life. The ability to dream or envision a goal is Spirit's divine plan to inspire us to reach and stretch beyond our human limitations. Most big goals, and some little goals, require us to partner with Spirit for their completion and success. Dreams are the longings Spirit placed inside us to help us maintain our connection to "It." You may see me interchange the word "It" for Spirit, to denote the impersonal nature of Spirit. Spirit does not have human attributes; however we may at times see humans display the attributes of Spirit like **Love (unconditional), Empathy, Peace, Harmony, Joy, Kindness, Compassion, Tranquility, Gentleness, Consolation, Understanding, Excellence and Creativity**.

There are people who genuinely do not want or need a romantic relationship. They are a small minority, but they exist and are happy on their own and naturally feel better that way. Then, the rest of us who want to have a partner need to be able to be happy and content on our own. There is the notion that a spouse or partner will make you happy, however that is not true. We have to make ourselves happy whether we are in or out of a relationship with someone. Another person can complement our happiness. If you can't be happy on your own you won't be happy in a relationship with others. I believe being alone or single is as natural as being in a couple, it's just that our society puts so much pressure on individuals to get coupled that they start feeling inadequate if they are not. I feel that this is where most of the single unhappiness comes from.

It is good for everyone to have periods of singleness, because we need to understand who we are as an individual, and it's much easier to do that when you are not in a relationship. Grow, get to know yourself, explore who you really are, what you want from life, what makes you happy and fulfilled. People who go from one relationship to another without breaks often have no idea who they are on their own, which is in my opinion an essential condition to be able to be truly happy with someone else as well.

Looking At Age, Through the Eyes of Love

The challenge we face in life is how we set ourselves up to fail with all our false beliefs about our self, life and the aging process. Aging is something beautiful, just as growing up is beautiful. We grow from a child, to a teenager, to a young woman or a young man. It is beautiful to become an old woman or an old man. In the life of humans, there are certain years where we actively reproduce. During those years, we are sexually attractive because nature makes us that way. After that, we do not have to be sexually attractive from that point of view; however it does not mean we are not beautiful.

You are what you believe you are. There is nothing you need to do except to be just what you are. You have the right to feel beautiful and enjoy it. You can honor your body and accept it as it is. You do not need any one to love you. Love comes from the inside. It lives inside us and is always there, but with our wall of fog about who we are we may not feel loving. You can only see and understand the beauty that lives outside you when you feel the love and beauty that lives inside you.

PRESS ON
Goethe

Nothing in the world can take the place of persistence.
Talent will not, nothing is more common, than unsuccessful
men with talent.
Genius will not; unrewarded genius is almost a proverb.
Education alone will not; the world is full of educated derelicts.
Persistence and determination alone are omnipotent.

How to Cope With the Loneliness
and Isolation of Success

The way we think and feel about ourselves is critical to how much energy, aliveness and joy we experience daily. If our mental state is preoccupied with worry, doubt, anger, hate or negative warped thinking, we are likely to experience both physical and mental fatigue. When we hate ourselves, disrespect ourselves, hold ourselves in contempt, have low self-worth or have low self-esteem, it affects our total being. To be successful in anything daily you need energy, aliveness, enthusiasm and joy.

Are you ready for success? If you were asked this question by an unsuspecting person more than likely your immediate reply would be a resounding "yes." Then the words, "why do you ask?" would probably flash across your mind or flow from your lips. Seldom if ever

78

will anyone ask you this question in your lifetime. Most of us are never questioned as to whether we are ready for success by anyone, including ourselves. It is little wonder that we lack motivation and drive for our goals. How can we ever marshal forth our inner resources to act if we have never asked the question of ourselves?

I am constantly being asked by people: How do you live alone? Are you not afraid to live by yourself? My secret weapon is that my mom introduced me to my Guardian Angel when I 5 or 6 years old. We had a large picture in our living room of a little boy and girl crossing a bridge with a plank missing on the bridge, and they did not fall into the river because they had a huge angel watching over them. She told me and my sister that wherever we went we had an angel watching over us. I had forgotten that in my conscious mind, however my unconscious mind, which records everything, remembered it. Later in my career when I worked as a counselor, the children always reported to me that they saw many angels, some as high as 30 angels. So I reignited my relationship with my many angels and started reading and studying about angels. I discovered that all adults have a Guardian and 12 other angels. I now do angel readings over the phone and in person. So you and I are never alone. I would ask you to entertain these thoughts: Are there angels on earth? I believe there are. Who and what is an EARTH ANGEL?

The pathways of angels are marked by beautiful moments, tender gestures and sweet gifts to the soul. The mark of an angel is lightness, joy, tranquility, love, patience, unconditional positive regard and freedom from judgment of others.

LOVE

Seek an angel with an open heart, and you shall always find one.

The only way to know an angel is through your feelings.

Angels may not always come when you call them, but they come when you need them.

An angel is someone who helps you believe in miracles again.

Sometimes you know angels only by the miracles they leave blossoming in their path after they are gone.

An angel is someone you're always very happy to bump into.

An angel is someone who raises your spirits.

An angel is someone you feel you've known forever even though you've just met.

An angel is anyone who helps you grow.

Angels make you feel welcome in this world.

Angels encourage your best qualities and hidden talents.

Angels give you those gentle pats on the back, you sometimes need to keep going.

Angels give you direction.

Angels gently push you out of your little self and into the broad arena of love.

Angels remind you that you are enough.

Angels help you see your life in a better light.

An angel is someone who brings out the angel in you.

COMMITMENT
Goethe

Until one is committed there is hesitancy,
The chance to draw back,
Always ineffectiveness,
Concerning all acts of initiative
And creating there is one elementary truth,
The ignorance of which kills countless ideas
And splendid plans;
The moment one definitely commits oneself,
All sorts of things begin to happen that would
 Never otherwise have occurred
A whole stream of events issues from
The committed decision,
Raising in one's favor all matter of incidents,
Meetings and material assistance,
Which no (wo)man could have dreamed
Would come his/ her way
Whatever you can do, or dream you can do, begin it.
Boldness has genius, power and magic in it.

Come To The Edge
Guillaume Apollinaire

Life said, come to the edge
They said, we can't, we will fall.

Come to the edge, life said.
They came, life pushed them…
And they flew.

Motivational Reminders

Motivation fuels the fire within…again, attitude about life's setbacks and not the setbacks themselves determine success.

1. Once you make a choice, it then makes you.

2. In order for change to occur on the outside, it must first occur on the inside.

3. Choosing today, changes tomorrow.

4. Successful people fail more than failures do.

5. You will miss 100 percent of the shots you don't take.

6. Knowledge enables, empowers and endorses success.

7. There are few feelings greater than feeling that we control our desires, rather than allowing our desires to control us.

8. Your strengths are seen in what you stand for, your weaknesses in what you fall for.

9. A temporary commitment cannot solve a long-term problem.

10. If you don't control your life, your life will control you.

11. Learn to experience the momentary pain of discipline, rather than the lasting pain of regret.

12. You can't change where you've been, but you can change where you're going.

13. People generally fail not because they're defeated, but because they quit.

14. You were not created to fail; you were created to succeed.

15. Your work will pay off; it's not a matter of if, but when.

16. The goal you set today will be the reward you receive tomorrow.

17. Success lies in your ability to look beyond the challenge and focus on the goal.

18. If you don't schedule your time, time will schedule you.

19. Physical and spiritual fitness provide the energy to deal with life's challenges, the strength to press through and the ability to continue regardless of circumstances.

20. Poor choices take us farther than we want to go, keep us longer than we want to stay and cost us more than we want to pay.

21. Don't get discouraged. It's not the fall that hurts; it's staying down that does.

22. Success is determined by the ability to take action, failure by the inability to take action.

23. Desire will find a way; excuses hide the way.

24. Thoughts become words, words become actions, actions become habits and habits become a lifestyle.

25. Putting first things first leads to success.

26. Take the safest route, not the fastest.

27. Those who succeed walk through adversity, not without it.

28. Success in weight loss is 10 percent circumstance, 90 percent attitude.

29. Never look back unless it's the direction you want to go.

30. A true measure of a person is not what they were, but what they will become.

31. The obstacles ahead are never as great as the power behind.

32. Don't let someone's opinion of you become your reality.

33. Your life is a reflection of the choices you make.

I Am There
James Dillet Freeman

Do you need Me? I am there.
You cannot see Me, yet I am the light you see by.
You cannot hear Me, yet I speak through your voice.
You cannot feel Me, yet I am the power at work in your hands.

I am at work, though you do not understand My ways.
I am at work, though you do not recognize My works.
I am not strange visions. I am not mysteries.

Only in absolute stillness, beyond self, can you know Me as I am, and then but as a feeling and a faith.
Yet I am there. Yet I hear. Yet I answer.

When you need Me, I am there.
Even if you deny Me, I am there.
Even when you feel most alone, I am there.
Even in your fears, I am there.
Even in your pain, I am there.
I am there when you pray and when you do not pray.
I am in you, and you are in Me.

Only in your mind can you feel separate from Me, for only in your mind are the mists of "yours" and "mine."
Yet only with your mind can you know Me and experience Me.
Empty your heart of empty fears.
When you get yourself out of the way, I am there.
You can of yourself do nothing, but I can do all. And I am in all.

Though you may not see the good, good is there, for I am there.
I am there, because I have to be, because I am.
Only in Me does the world have meaning; only out of Me does the world go forward.
I am the law on which the movement of the stars and the growth of living cells are founded.
I am the love that is the law's fulfilling.
I am assurance.
I am peace.
I am oneness.
I am the law that you can live by.
I am the love that you can cling to.
I am your assurance.
I am your peace.
I am one with you. I am.
Though you fail to find Me, I do not fail you.

Though your faith in Me is unsure, My faith in you never wavers,
because I know you, because I love you.
Beloved, I am there.

Leave Trails for Others to Follow
Anonymous

Leave traditions that are timeless which pass our faith to the next generation.
Roots that are rich in heritage that will firmly develop our children's spiritual and moral character.

Attitudes which are angelic in nature's inspiration to build a bridge for others to cross,

Legacy of love for our sons and daughters; And strength to continue the journey

The Business of Friendship
Unknown

The happiest business in the world is that of making friends,
And no "Investment" on "the Street" pays larger dividends.
For life is more than stocks and bonds and love than rate percent
And he who gives in friendship's name, shall reap as she has spent.
Life is the great investment and no man lives in vain,
Who guards a hundred friendships, as misers guard their gain.
Then give the world a welcome each day whatever forecloses the partnership of friends.

How to Accept Being Alone

We all need quiet time for our spirit to evolve, and we need quiet time to be alone so that Spirit can speak to us and through us. Many of us are afraid to be alone because we are afraid of our thoughts. Some of us are afraid to think because we have negative thoughts about ourselves, have low self-esteem, low self-worth and only have worth in relation to people outside ourselves. It is good to know whether you are an inner directed or outer directed person. If you are an inner directed person, you may not like being alone because you are shy, introverted and have not learned the people skills necessary to project or promote yourself. I was once shy and unsure of myself as a teenager.

After I left home and went to college, I realized that I had to create a new family (my friends) if I wanted someone to talk to and with whom to spend time. I started to introduce myself to others and started a conversation with others, because I was feeling lonely for my family. This has happened to me on many occasions throughout my life.

The next time I was alone was when I moved to San Diego California as a young newlywed and my husband died after five years of marriage. That was scary and frightening to live in a city and not know anyone except the people I worked with. I had to make friends quickly. The first night after my husband died, I spent three nights at the home of one of my co-workers because I was afraid to be in the house by myself. I was still afraid so one of the nurses I worked with gave me a puppy to keep me company. I put him in a box right beside my bed, and I slept like a baby, and I have slept peacefully from then on. Now once my head hits the bed, I go into a deep sleep and do not awaken until the alarm clock goes off, or when I choose to sleep until I get enough sleep and awaken naturally.

As a teenager I was bitten by a dog and was afraid of dogs; however, this one was a puppy who needed a family, like me, and I no longer felt alone. I continue to work on my desire to be with people rather than enjoying my own company. We are socialized to feel there is something wrong with us if we are not surrounded by people or engaging in a conversation with people.

This past Labor Day holiday, I wanted to experience fulfillment. I made a decision to not call anyone on the phone and to talk to someone only if they called me on the phone. I live alone in San Diego California, so I normally call my family members to say hi. It seemed odd and strange. Because of my desire to connect, I normally call all of my family members. This time I enjoyed my own company, and I enjoyed looking at the tree in my front yard. I swam in my pool two times, once in the morning and again in the late evening. I gave thanks to Spirit for allowing me to swim in my own pool for 30 years. There are very few people who have the use of their limbs and have the energy to swim for that many years. Living alone and being alone is a good thing if you want to get to know your inner "Divine" self on a deeper level.

I have lived with two husbands; however, I have lived alone for the last 25 years and I have enjoyed my time living alone. I certainly have gotten more accomplished by living alone, because I have been able to create my own schedule whenever and however I want to. I don't need to worry or concern myself that I was ignoring someone or avoiding taking into consideration the needs or welfare of someone else, and I had the freedom to do so. I felt power in my freedom to create my day as I desired.

I decided I would not marry or date another man until I figured out what caused me to be attracted to a man with an abusive personality. I discovered that I love taking care of people, being the compassionate caretaker that I was and am. I had a high tolerance for a sob story and gave people, especially men, too many chances to correct their behavior. I have learned during the past 26 years how to live alone without a man or feeling that I needed a man to make me feel whole or complete as a woman. I still love men and find them attractive; however, I do not bring home stray men, stray dogs or stray cats to fill the void of my alone time. I can now be happy with or without a man in my life, and I am open to allow myself to have a healthy male/ female relationship without verbal or emotional abuse.

Now I am aware of who I am and what is my "life's purpose". My purpose is to love, to heal, to serve and to begin this process of transformation for me and everyone who enters my life. I am no longer afraid to live alone. Life is to embraced with joy, to be lived with passion, to be shared with someone with whom we can easily communicate, who is looking in the same direction for their life purpose as us, someone who has our same vision for tranquility, peace, family, laughter, someone who can harmonize our energy, help calm our fears, our anxieties when we need up lifting and who will love and accept us as we are. If that person is nowhere in sight, then I suggest you become the loving, caring, compassionate, gentle, spiritual, communicative person you want to have in your life. It all starts with you. Be the love you want to have in your life. You are with you 24 hours a day and no one knows you better than you.

So help yourself to better understand who you are and what are your likes, dislikes, your weakness, your strengths, what you can tolerate and what you are unwilling to tolerate to be in a relationship. Be more self-aware and less judgmental of others. I know I am into judgment of another person when they react to something I say. Do not allow yourself to live with tolerations of any kind, especially tolerations that destroy your soul like anger, resentment, confusion, fear, anxiety, disagreeable people, power and control, you holding a negative attitude, verbal, physical or emotional abuse or a fear of loss or being alone. All of these affect your spirit of play, your spirit of joy, your spirit of peace, your peace and your love of life and living.

Keep looking inside yourself, for it is there that you will find the answers to all of your problems and challenges in life. Learn to love yourself and others will love you. Others always treat us as we treat ourselves. Life is lived from the inside out. Everything that you will ever need is deep within your soul. Find a way to better know who you are, what drives you and what makes you happy. Find a way to give back to the world. We are here to be a blessing to someone other than ourselves. We are the eyes, hands, feet and words of the Great Divine Spirit. Let your life and your service to humanity become a light unto the world. For you will live this particular life you are now living with all its splendor and glory only this one time.

Let your life count; let it be a life, well lived. Let it end with an exclamation point rather than with a comma or period. Let your time on planet earth have meaning; let it speak to the pain and suffering you helped to heal including your own pain and suffering. Ask not what you can get from life but what you can give. Ask how you can be a part of the solution rather than a part of the problem. Learn to quiet you mind, so that you do not complain and criticize yourself or others. Learn to find a way to uplift the spirit of someone on a daily basis, starting with you. We were born to be both, in relationship with another person, and to be alone. We came into this world alone and we will leave alone. They only put one person in a casket, a burial plot or in a cremation urn.

Because you have purchased this book, you are entitled to receive a complimentary Self Love Evaluation session. I am a Self-Love Intuitive Life Coach. If I can serve you in any way Go to: www.journeytoselflove.com by E-mail: ida@thejourneytoselflove.com, www.idagreene.com www.greatnesstravel.com

Reflections

Learn to embrace change.
Become your own best friend,
Practice patience,
Become friends with stillness and quietness.
Have faith in yourself and have faith in the goodness of others.
Be glad for the good of others and the universe will do the same for you.

The Thoughts You Think Today,
Create Your Tomorrows

References

1. Apter AJ, Garcia LA, Boyd RC, Xingmei Wang, Bogen DK, MD, PhD, Ten Have T. "Exposure to community violence is associated with asthma hospitalizations and emergency department visits." *The Journal of Allergy and Clinical Immunology*, September 2010, 126/3: 552-57

2. Suglia SF, Enlow MB, Kullowatz A, Wright R J. (2009). "Maternal intimate partner violence and increased asthma incidence in children: Buffering effects of supportive caregiving." *Archives of Pediatrics & Adolescent Medicine*, 163(3): 244-250.

3. Wright RJ, Mitchell H, Visness CM, Cohen S, Stout J, Evans R, MD, Gold DR. "Community Violence and Asthma Morbidity: The Inner-City Asthma Study." *American Journal of Public Health*, April 2004, Vol 94, No. 4: 625-63.

4. Sternthal MJ, Jun HJ, Earls F, Wright RJ. "Community violence and urban childhood asthma: a multilevel analysis." *European Respiratory Review*, December 1, 2010, 36(6): 1400-1409.

5. Wright RJ, Steinbach SF. "Violence: an unrecognized environmental exposure that may contribute to greater asthma morbidity in high risk inner-city populations." *Environmental Health Perspectives,* 2001 October, 109(10): 1085-1089.

6. Fujiwara T. "Violence and Asthma: A Review." *Environmental Health Insights*, 2008:2: 45-54.

About the Author

Dr. Ida Greene is a Self-Love Coach, Motivational Speaker, Licensed Marriage, Family, Child Therapist, Ordained Minister, Registered Nurse, Travel Agent, and Author of 22 best-selling books. She is also an Intuitive Healer, Reiki Energy Practitioner, Actor, and founder of Center of Self-Esteem, whose mission is to end violence and abuse of women and children. She speaks and provides training on: 7 Keys To Master Self Love, and Mastering Your Personal Power.

Dr. Greene received the NAWBO "BRAVO" award, "Best Humanitarian Campaign", Book Publicist of Southern California, Writers Notes Book Award for her book *Anger Management Skills for Children*, San Diego Business Journal, Multicultural Heritage Award, and Book Expo America Self-Publisher of the year award.

She is a frequent radio talk show guest, and can be reached for Keynote or Motivational presentations. She was listed in the book *100 Plus Most Admired African Women in Literature* and her article on Stress Management was published in *"ALL" Magazine*.

Dr. Greene Coaches on "How to Be Alone, Without Feeling Lonely", "Looking for Love, In All the Wrong Places" and helps you Master Your Personal Power on Your Journey to Self-Love, through her Journey to Self-Love Coaching, Workshops and Retreats.

To get your Complimentary Self Love Evaluation session go to: www.journeytoselflove.com
E-mail: ida@thejourneytoselflove.com.
www.idagreene.com , www.greatnesstravel.com

Our books are available at www.idagreeene.com, Amazon, and Barnes and Noble.

Journey to Self-Love Coaching, Workshops & Retreats

Dr. Ida Greene shares her magical strategies with people through Speaking Journey to Self-Love Coaching Workshops, Webinar, Tele-Summits, Trainings, and Retreats. Dr. Ida is available as an Inspirational Keynote Speaker, and Motivational Speaker. The goal is to help you move through the barriers that keep you from being your best in your personal and professional life.

She is a highly gifted Intuitive Healer, providing: Clairaudient Messages, Past Life Regressions, Energy Clearing, Angel Readings, and Reiki Energy balancing sessions by phone appointments, 619-262-9951.

Dr. Greene coaches on "How to Be Alone, Without Feeling Lonely", "Looking for Love, In All the Wrong Places" and helps you Master Your Personal Power on Your Journey to Self-Love, through her Journey to Self-Love Coaching, Workshops and Retreats.

To get your Complimentary Self Love Evaluation session go to: www.journeytoselflove.com

E-mail: ida@thejourneytoselflove.com.
www.idagreene.com , www.greatnesstravel.com

Our books are available at www.idagreeene.com, Amazon, and Barnes and Noble.